# A WORLD OF OPPORTUNITIES FOR ASPIRING ENTREPRENEURS

## CREATING YOUR OWN JOB

## IN THE "NEW NORMAL"

Greg Smogard, PhD

4catalysts consulting

4catalysts consulting trade paperback edition, 2013
ISBN: 0615709850
ISBN 13: 9780615709857

Library of Congress Control Number: 2012956477

# Dedication

*This book is dedicated to my parents, Ken and Terry, whose love, support, and tolerance provided the basis for my perspective on the world. And to the angels in my life, Laura, Danielle, and Ashley, who surround me with their love and show me every day what is truly important in life.*

# Acknowledgments

Many individuals, companies, organizations, and institutions indirectly contributed to this book. My former Fortune 500 employers trained me in the fields of financial services, entertainment, and retail, and they gave me the opportunity to travel the world and learn how business is done globally. Additionally, my former and current business and start-up clients taught me and teach me every day how creative, hardworking, innovative people need to continually adapt to address the accelerating rate of change in their business models.

Individually, I would like to thank two dear friends and occasional business partners who have always provided wise and constructive feedback: Fernando Amandi, whose career and life have paralleled mine for decades—from the snow-covered peaks of the Chilean Andes to various business experiences—always inspires me with his eloquent, thought-provoking perspectives and personal courage, and Dr. Miguel Nunez, who is not only a professional and caring physician but also a wise businessman.

I would also like to thank Rachel Marie Burke, who proofread the book and fact-checked all of my endnotes, which was no small task. Her attention to detail, her background in management consulting, and her transition to graduate work in medicine attests to her vast talent, and I was delighted to receive her input.

I would also like to acknowledge that taking on this topic and the trends associated with it was difficult on a couple of levels.

First, writing my first book while consulting full-time extended the experience to a couple of years. Second, this meant that many of the trends, the economic numbers—and, in some cases, even the methodology and definitions—were always changing. As a one-person operation with no research team, I found that tracking, updating, citing, and adapting to changing data was very challenging. It is my intent to be as accurate as possible and cite the correct sources for all information. However, I acknowledge that errors and omissions might exist, and I would hope that in the true collaborative, crowdsourcing spirit, readers would point them out so these issues can be corrected. That being said, I hope in a small way that this book will inspire some individuals and/or companies, to identify an opportunity and to consider launching a new, full-time or part-time venture that will create more jobs for all of us in this new normal.

# Table of Contents

**Part One:** WHY: Structural Shifts & Employment in the New Normal    **1**

Issue 1    Business & Finance:    US Employment: The New Normal    3
Issue 2    Business & Finance:    The Real Unemployment Rate    9
Issue 3    Business & Finance:    Manufacturing & Consumer Spending    15
Issue 4    Business & Finance:    Automation & Outsourcing    19
Issue 5    Business & Finance:    Housing & Income Distribution    25

**Part Two:** HOW: Entrepreneurial "Engines of Growth"—Again    **33**

Issue 6    Culture & Society:    The Age of the Individual    35
Issue 7    Business & Finance:    The Entrepreneurial Revolution    41
Issue 8    Science & Technology:    The Innovation/Usefulness Gap    47
Issue 9    Culture & Society:    The 1% Innovation & Entrepreneur Fund    51

**Part Three:** WHAT: US Issues & Trends for Entrepreneurs & Disruptors    **59**

Issue 10    Education:    High School Graduation Rates    61
Issue 11    Demographics & Markets:    The Baby Boomer Market    67
Issue 12    Environment:    Extreme Weather    71
Issue 13    Demographics & Markets:    Habla Español?    77
Issue 14    Science & Technology:    Disruptive Innovation    83
Issue 15    Health:    Healthcare: New Ideas Needed—Stat    89
Issue 16    Culture & Society:    The Age of Thrift    93
Issue 17    Demographics & Markets:    Local Food    99
Issue 18    Business & Finance:    Web & Mobile Business    105
Issue 19    Culture & Society:    Co-ops, Barter, P2P, & Crowd Sourcing    111
Issue 20    Demographics & Markets:    Cities & Towns—Reinvent Yourselves    117
Issue 21    Demographics & Markets:    Customer Relationships—The Core of Your Business?    123
Issue 22    Culture & Society:    Big Challenges—Big Ideas—Big Opportunities    131

**Part Four:** WHAT: Global Issues & Trends    **137**

Issue 23    Business & Finance:    Global Unemployment    139
Issue 24    Business & Finance:    Top 10 Entrepreneurial Nations    145
Issue 25    Environment:    Water Management    149
Issue 26    Demographics & Markets:    Brazil—Emerging Middle Class & World-Class Events    155
Issue 27    Business & Finance:    Global Competitiveness    161
Issue 28    Demographics & Markets:    Markets at the Bottom of the Pyramid    165
Issue 29    Culture & Society:    Social Entrepreneurs    169
Issue 30    Science & Technology:    India & China: Emerging Giants    173

# Introduction

I wrote this book as a catalyst for interested individuals to consider becoming full-time or part-time entrepreneurs and innovators, and I wrote it to identify US and global trends that represent potential opportunities for entrepreneurs. Whether we like it or not, the world is changing quickly. Certain politicians, institutions, organizations, and even companies are either unable or unwilling to adapt to this changing world. The federal government has become paralyzed due to its growing polarization, inefficiency, and inability to generate consensus to solve even the most basic issues. Now that the 2012 presidential election is over, we will evaluate whether and which of these private and public sector players can begin to collaborate, invest, and provide the leadership needed to continue to develop and to support the innovative environment and entrepreneurial infrastructure required to help create the next wave of critical, well-paying jobs.

Given the speed and complexity of global change, an ineffective or immobilized government can no longer be one of the major, innovative engines of job growth, as it had been during key periods of our history. Even multinational corporations, while sitting on record cash reserves, remain uncertain about the economy and the US business environment.

Now, several years into the jobless economic recovery, a significant gap has developed between those with consistent, well-paying jobs and the growing number of unemployed and underemployed. Despite gradual improvement in specific sectors of the economy, other sectors have experienced reduced investment and eliminated jobs, leaving many talented and hardworking individuals without the opportunity to replace their lost income, benefits, and job security. The harsh truth is that many of these jobs will not be coming back, and those who are directly affected and displaced need to consider alternatives, such as retraining, switching industries, pursuing contract or part-time work, or, in some cases, becoming entrepreneurs.

Many writers have referred to this new era as a "paradigm shift" or the "new normal." Whatever the phrase, the rules are changing, and we need to adapt to them—and quickly. We can no longer just depend on traditional employers to provide all of our jobs. We must become more informed and proactive. We need to create many of our own employment opportunities. To do that, we need to get smarter, more innovative, and more entrepreneurial.

I wrote this book with three purposes.

1. First, to communicate my view that the prolonged, weak economic recovery is not just another cyclical episode brought on by a housing crisis and credit derivative trading gone wild, but rather a stark reminder of some of the structural shifts that the US economy has been experiencing for decades. These shifts individually and cumulatively, have contributed to increased long-term unemployment, decreased buying power for certain households, and a growing income distribution gap. If consumer spend less it can lead to less business profits, and this leads to less investment, less hiring, and then less spending again.

2. Second, I wrote this book to suggest that one solution for job creation is for voluntary and involuntary entrepreneurs to launch millions of new, innovative full-time and part-time startups and small businesses, which can become the new engines of

growth. The US has been and continues to be a global leader in entrepreneurship and innovation, but given the economic and political challenges we face in this new normal, we need to significantly improve our commitment and expand and scale our infrastructure, funding, and capabilities. This time around, much of the effort will need to come from the bottom up, and it will need to come from individuals like us.

3.  Finally, I wrote this book to provide summary information to potential entrepreneurs, disruptive innovators, businesspeople, and students regarding various US and global trends that represent market needs and potential opportunities.

The book is divided into four parts.

Part One briefly summarizes several structural economic issues that were exacerbated by the 2007–2009 recession and continue to plague the jobless recovery. Some of these issues have been gradually affecting our lives for decades. Many individuals in the US and worldwide are experiencing profound changes in their work, standard of living, healthcare, education, financial status, society, retirement, and global competitiveness. Despite the so-called recovery, many countries are still faced with stubbornly high unemployment rates. It's apparent that people cannot continue to wait for governments, institutions, organizations, and companies to replace all of those lost high-paying jobs and benefits packages. The time has come for some of us to create our own jobs by generating new ideas and/or enhanced business models. Innovation is the key, and much of it will come from the bottom up. These changes provide both challenges and opportunities. The way that you understand, accept, and react to this rapid change may determine which side of the equation that you are on.

Part Two discusses issues related to the convergence of timing and opportunity. This is a good time for individuals to consider joining the entrepreneurial revolution. Although both the US and the global entrepreneurial infrastructures need improvement, the tools available to aspiring entrepreneurs and innovators are myriad and growing daily. Additionally, the so-called usefulness gap between sophisticated technology developments and the basic needs of the average consumer is expanding quickly, which opens the door for more disruptive business opportunities. Finally, I propose a challenge for the US public and private sectors to cooperate in doubling the number of full-time and part-time startups in two years, which could help jump-start a solid and sustainable economic recovery.

Parts Three (US) and Four (International) focus on miscellaneous issues that I believe represent potential opportunities for entrepreneurs and innovators. Part Three identifies macro trends, challenges, and opportunities that are relevant to the US but not exclusive to it. Part Four concentrates on globalization and the importance of global citizens, businesses, and entrepreneurs understanding international trends. Globalization involves much more than the outsourcing of jobs or free trade. Today there are very few things in our lives that are not dependent on global events or issues. Understanding globalization and its relationship to you, your family, your job—or lack thereof—and your community is no longer a luxury. It has now become a necessity.

I have included thirty issues for your consideration. Each issue is a quick read that is intended to provoke your thinking. The issues are grouped into one of seven broad sectors to help you easily navigate to the areas of your particular interest:

**Business & Finance**
**Culture & Society**
**Demographics & Markets**
**Education**
**The Environment**
**Health**
**Science & Technology**

Each issue is then divided into six smaller sections to help stimulate your thinking:

| | |
|---|---|
| **Issue:** | A brief description |
| **Opportunity:** | A quick look at a potential opportunity |
| **Example:** | A specific example |
| **Entrepreneurs & Disruptors:** | Idea starters |
| **Mix & Match:** | Apply your unique talents to the specific issue |
| **Your Ideas:** | Your space |

I hope you enjoy this book. Let me know what you think at newnormal@4catalysts.com.

# Part One

WHY: STRUCTURAL SHIFTS & EMPLOYMENT
IN THE NEW NORMAL

# Issue 1:   US Employment: The New Normal

Sector:    Business & Finance

Location:  US

## Issue: Structural Unemployment

The media is full of reports about the job crisis in the US and around the world. Almost four years after the Great Recession and we have only been able to replace a small portion of all of those precious lost jobs. Why not? Has something fundamentally changed regarding job creation? The answers are complex and are comprised of both short-term issues and long-term trends. Since we have become increasingly focused on short-term business results and 24/7 media reporting, the unemployment issue frequently gets explained in political terms or that businesses are reluctant to hire due to economic or tax uncertainty, rising healthcare costs or difficulty in matching labor force skills with open positions. All of these issues are real and represent barriers to hiring, however, I believe it is helpful to look at some structural trends that have also contributed to the current employment new normal.

The US economy is evolving due to several structural factors. Many of these factors are not new but have been ongoing for decades. These factors are creating a paradigm shift in how we work and how much we earn, which affect how much we spend and how much businesses grow and hire.

The recession, which began in December of 2007 and lasted until June of 2009, was the longest recession since World War II[1]. Its effects have been prolonged, and as with each recent recession, the economy is taking increasingly longer to bounce back. This is happening because the downturn is not strictly a short-term or cyclical event.

Here is a list of the months required for employment to return to pre-downturn levels:

| Downturn | Months required |
|----------|-----------------|
| 1981–82 | 28 |
| 1990–91 | 32 |
| 2001 | 46 |
| 2007–09 | **63** and counting (April, 2013)[2] |

One consequence of the recession and the anemic recovery is the persistently high rate of general and long-term unemployment, which negatively impacts discretionary income and consumer spending. According to statistics from the Bureau of Labor Statistics, the US economy has lost 7 million jobs since the beginning of the recession[3].

Unless you are happily employed and comfortably compensated in the new normal you are probably experiencing changes in your work, salary, benefits, standard of living, healthcare costs, purchasing power, retirement, educational opportunities, and/or global competitiveness. These changes can be challenging.

Like a trip to the doctor to diagnose an ailment, we must first identify and consider the symptoms before we can apply a remedy. If you are one of the following, you are likely having a problem getting a full-time job, or if you have gotten one, it may not offer the salary or the benefits that you had hoped for:

- An executive in transition
- Someone over the age of forty-five
- A college graduate from the class of 2009 to the present
- Someone without a high school diploma
- Someone who is considered long-term unemployed

Some of the long-term structural factors influencing this new normal are:

- **High and persistent long-term unemployment rates**
- **The ongoing transition from a manufacturing economy to a service and knowledge economy**
- **Declining income & declining consumer spending**
- **Globalization**
- **Increased automation**
- **Jobs being moved overseas**
- **Productivity enhancements**
- **Industry consolidation**
- **The housing crisis**
- **A growing income distribution gap**

Each of these will be briefly addressed in the next sections.

## Example: Age & Unemployment

At the beginning of 2013, the average (mean) period of unemployment for those fifty-five years old and older was just slightly more than one year[4]. Because this group is generally more skilled and experienced, they are generally more highly paid. Consequently, the loss of many of these older, valuable employees creates a brain drain that represents a risk to knowledge transfer and competitiveness. This loss, however, could be someone else's gain.

Currently, there is a surplus of highly skilled and experienced experts in the job market. If you are one of those individuals and you believe that you have the right skill sets, motivation, and funding, it may be time to consider becoming a full-time or part-time entrepreneur. If you are an employer, you need to revisit this talent pool and maybe gain a competitive or innovative edge and a very experienced employee.

# Entrepreneurs & Disruptors: Manufacturing

High-paying manufacturing jobs in the US have been trending downward for years, and they have been increasingly impacted by the most recent recessions. Between 1949 and 2011, the manufacturing sector lost an average of 7.8 percent of its jobs. Since 2000, that number has increased to 12.4 percent and jumped to 16.3 percent during the last recession[5]. This decline is critical since manufacturing has been the base for many high-paying middle-class jobs that provide the consumer spending to drive both the US and global economies. The good news is that, as of late, the sector has been bouncing back.

One of my favorite TV shows is the Science Channel's *How It's Made*. Although this show highlights the automation of the manufacturing industry, which ironically is responsible for some of the structural unemployment in the sector, it also depicts the genius involved in making things. For entrepreneurs, innovators, and disruptors, leveraging this brilliance into new or retooled product lines is a critical path to recapturing both high-paying jobs and America's manufacturing leadership.

One solution to our unemployment dilemma is **Innovation + Manufacturing**. Innovation alone cannot be the only solution, since many ideas—solar panels, for example—are designed in the US and then shipped overseas for development and manufacturing. The US must get back to making things so that both the ideas and the products are invented and manufactured here.

Another great TV show for entrepreneurs is CNN's *Next List*. In a recent episode, they highlighted a company called TechShop, which, for a membership fee, allows creative entrepreneurs and innovators access to tools and equipment to experiment and actually make their own designs and prototypes. They have been so successful that they are opening up shops around the country. They are also working with the Veterans Administration to supply memberships to returning war veterans. Bravo! Check them out at www.techshops.ws.

## Mix & Match

Do you have skills that contribute to or are dependent on manufacturing techniques and processes? Mix and Match the skills and applications below or add your own skills to create job options.

Example: Packaging + Electronics + Sustainability = redesigning packaging to recycle or reduce waste

Skill:
Assembly
Engineering
Machinist
Quality Control
Product Design
Tool & Die Making
Packaging
Safety
Testing

Application:
Industry
Product
Service
Process

## Your Ideas:

## Issue 2:   The Real Unemployment Rate

Sector:    Business & Finance

Location:   US

## Issue: The Rate Is Higher Than You Think

To assess the impact of joblessness in the US, we need to understand the real unemployment rate. There is confusion between the "official" rate and the total number of unemployed and underemployed Americans. Many people are increasingly frustrated and fearful about the difficulty in finding a job and the weak economic recovery. If consumer confidence declines then reduced consumer spending cannot be far behind. If your business is not keeping pace with the political and media reporting of the recovery, or if you are seeing fewer consumers and less spending in your business or on your website, look behind the numbers for one possible explanation.

The unemployment rate typically reported in the media is not the whole story. Since its peak of 10 percent in October of 2009, the seasonally-adjusted unemployment rate has declined to 7.6 percent as of March, 2013[1]. The process used by the Bureau of Labor Statistics (BLS) is complicated and multi-faceted due to the challenging nature of calculating the unemployment rate. It simply defines three categories:

Employed—This includes people who have paying jobs.

Unemployed—This includes people who are jobless but available to work and have actively looked for work in the last four weeks.

Not in the Labor Force—This is the wild card that is responsible for understating the real unemployment and underemployment rates. To account for this segment, the government produces the U-6 or "alternative measures of labor underutilization" report.

To understand the differences in employment rates, you can see the definitions in the two key BLS indicators. In March of 2013, the indicators were:

**7.6%**   U-3—"Official Unemployment Rate": This is the seasonally adjusted total unemployed as a percentage of the total labor force.

**13.9%** U-6—This includes a) "discouraged workers" or those who want a job and are available to work but have become frustrated with the job search and are not currently looking; b) "people marginally attached to the labor force," or those who want a job, have actively looked for work in the last twelve months, and are available to work; and c) "part-time workers" or those who want to work full-time but have taken part-time jobs for economic reasons. This group is also referred to as the underemployed[2].

The U-6 indicator represents an additional 10 million Americans who are either unemployed or underemployed. Their lack of income and spending has been under-reported, but the economic impact is significant and real. Another BLS indicator to look at to measure employment in the US is the labor force participation rate which peaked in 2001, at slightly more than 67% and currently sits at 63.3%[2].

## Example: The Demographics of Unemployment

Not everyone is equally affected by unemployment, as indicated by the rates of unemployment in certain demographic segments.

## Duration of Unemployment[3]

| | |
|---|---|
| 27 weeks or more | 44% of all unemployed (5.3 million people) |

| **Occupation[4]** | **Unemployment Rate** |
|---|---|
| Construction | 14.3% |
| Agriculture & related jobs | 10.8% |

## Ethnicity[5, 6]

| | |
|---|---|
| African-American | 12.8% |
| Hispanic | 9.5% |
| White | 6.9% |
| Asian | 5.0% |

(April, 2013-not seasonally adjusted)

| **States[7]** | **Highest** | **Lowest** | |
|---|---|---|---|
| Nevada | 9.7% | N. Dakota | 3.3% |
| Illinois | 9.5% | Nebraska | 3.8% |
| California | 9.4% | S. Dakota | 4.1% |
| Mississippi | 9.4% | Iowa | 4.3% |

(March, 2013-not seasonally adjusted)

# Entrepreneurs & Disruptors: "Involuntary" Entrepreneurs

Many unemployed and underemployed people who become entrepreneurs out of necessity are frequently referred to as involuntary entrepreneurs. Self-employment is not their first choice, but they often transition into the world of entrepreneurs, innovators, and disruptors because of their limited job options, their desire to test a new idea, or family members, friends, and partners convincing them to pursue something innovative. **Becoming an entrepreneur can be risky and is not for everyone.** However, for many unemployed people, becoming an entrepreneur provides another option.

11

To hedge your bets, become more informed and educated about starting your own business. There is a vast array of excellent tools, organizations, individuals and how-to information available. If you have an idea, some funding, and the skills to launch it, try working on your idea part-time on weekends or evenings to test the concept!

## Mix & Match: Unmet Customer Needs

To develop an idea and/or business concept, combine unmet customer needs with your unique skill sets.

List businesses you know that:

- Provide poor service or products
- Alienate their customers
- Ignore customer segments because they are too small, unique, difficult, or undiscovered
- Fail to develop new products or services to meet or create changing customer demand

Now list your unique skill sets or knowledge that you could use to compete with or improve upon vulnerable business models:

- Industry training
- Product or service focus
- Process/productivity improvement
- Education and talents
- Interests and hobbies

# Your Ideas:

# Issue 3:    Manufacturing & Consumer Spending

Sector:      Business & Finance
Location:    US

## Issue: From Manufacturing to Services and Information

The US economy has transitioned through many phases in its
development. From agriculture to cottage manufacturing, commodities,
heavy industry, government spending, and international trade, the
economy has continued to diversify. Additionally, the US has also
grown accustomed to global leadership in many of these areas.
However, we have gradually been experiencing structural shifts in
our engines of growth away from higher-paying jobs to lower-paid,
contractor, service, and information jobs.

The loss of our manufacturing horsepower has been occurring for
decades (see Issue 1: New Normal). Since 1979, the economy has lost
over 8 million manufacturing jobs and billions of dollars in wages.
Much of this happened in the last decade[1]. There are several reasons
for these job losses, which I will address later, but one issue was the
gradual transitioning of jobs overseas by large companies. The concept
was that Americans could enjoy less-expensive products that were
made more cheaply abroad or through productivity enhancements at
home. The companies could then replace those lost jobs through new
R&D-generated businesses. The second part of that plan has not kept
pace with the first part, which contributes to a vicious cycle.

**Fewer jobs + lower wages and benefits + higher expenses + less credit = less consumer spending = decline in business revenue = less hiring = fewer jobs**

One solution to this problem is to reactivate and significantly expand the innovative spirit and infrastructure needed to maintain America's global leadership. During each phase of America's economic development, entrepreneurs flourished by developing and commercializing ideas. Although some individuals built large corporations, it has been the small business owners and entrepreneurs who have provided the backbone of the American economy.

## Example: Lower Pay & Credit Binges

If you have recently been active in the job market, you may have become aware that many of the jobs that are currently being created come with lower pay and fewer benefits, while healthcare, education, and energy prices have been increasing. Since the 1970s, income inequality has been gradually growing in the US with the percentage of household income generally decling for many American workers[2]. One would assume that if your income was reduced then your buying power should have slowed accordingly; however, this was not necessarily always the case.

So, if many households experienced reduced income, how could the US have enjoyed such a robust economic period during the last couple of decades? One answer is credit: credit cards, mortgages, low interest loans, lines of credit, home equity, and school loans, etc. Despite a decline in purchasing power, Americans spent much of the last three decades financing their purchases by embarking on a credit binge. Total household debt service as a percentage of personal disposable income grew significantly during this time[3]. When the housing crisis and the subsequent recession reduced access to credit, both borrowing and certain segments of consumer spending declined, as did the corresponding business revenue and hiring.

## Entrepreneurs & Disruptors: Underserved Markets & Unmet Customer Needs

Entrepreneurs, innovators and disruptors look for niche opportunities, underserved markets, and unmet customer needs. Where do you see potential convergence points between niche opportunities and the ideas, products, services, process improvements, or competitive advantages for creating high-paying jobs?

Critical function reliability
Complex problem-solving
Premium quality
Precision production
Dependability
Error-free performance
Breakthrough innovation
Specialized functionality
Supply-chain advantages
International expertise

## Mix & Match:

Once the convergence points between opportunities and ideas are identified, the question arises: who will pay how much for which product or service? When benefits are bigger, the prices may become higher. The buyers of these products or services are numerous. Match potential buyers below with the previous convergence points.

Small-sized or medium-sized businesses

Governments

Institutions

Multinational corporations

Organizations

Venture capital/private equity firms

## Your Ideas:

# Issue 4:   Automation & Outsourcing

Sector:    Business & Finance
Location:   US


## Issue:  Automation & Outsourcing

So, where have all of those high-paying jobs gone? Two of the answers can be found in automation and outsourcing trends.

Automating a job or using technology to replace repetitive human action is considered by many businesses to be a productivity enhancement. They have determined that it has become more cost-effective, efficient, and productive to use sophisticated software, computers, mobile and e-commerce platforms, precision machines, just-in-time inventory, custom manufacturing, multi-functional robots, analytics, self-service processes, and cloud computing. On the other hand, displaced workers may see automation as technology-driven job destruction. Based on our daily interactions with businesses we can quickly see that customer service reps. and checkout personnel among others, were the first victims. Any job that is easily transferable with little to no tradeoff in quality is vulnerable.

Besides improving productivity, businesses have also been driving down labor costs by moving jobs to lower-cost production centers outside of the US, a process known as outsourcing or off shoring. This process has also become associated with the term *globalization*. However, globalization is a much broader concept that highlights the growing interconnectedness of international markets and cultures. Today, capital, data, jobs, ideas, intellectual property, products, services, information, and people move around the globe faster than ever.

19

Moving jobs offshore to places like Mexico, India, China, Central America, Eastern Europe, Southeast Asia, and Africa has been going on for decades, due to declining barriers to conducting business abroad, a growing supply of skilled foreign workers and middle-class markets, and the constant search for lower-cost production options.

The reality for American workers is that both automation and job outsourcing are structural changes that have occurred from years of rapidly evolving technology and the emergence and integration of large global markets and labor forces. Automation and outsourcing are not just short-term, cyclical changes that resulted from the latest downturn.

## Example: Industry Consolidations & Multinational Markets

As I have seen throughout my business career, unemployment can also happen when joint ventures, mergers, and acquisitions occur and industries consolidate. One factor for M&A activity is the perceived cost savings, synergies, and/or efficiencies created by eliminating redundant positions or company divisions that are either underperforming or no longer have a strategic fit under the new regime. These lost jobs are not typically replaced. This industry consolidation phenomenon has been occurring for years. In some cases, it is obvious when a well-known brand name disappears. However, because of strong brand awareness and performance, many acquirers— whether competitors or private equity players—prefer to operate the acquired company under the original brand name. Consequently, if job losses occur during the integration process, it is not readily apparent to the public, since everything appears to be business as usual.

Many industries have been consolidating for some time. Some examples include:

Media—Many local radio, TV, and newspaper companies have been consolidated into a small group of global giants.

Banking—In the mid-1980s, there were over 14,000 banks and 3,500 savings institutions in the US. By 2010, through a combination of consolidations and failures, those numbers had fallen by 55 percent and 68 percent, respectively[1].

Food—The top four firms in the world account for over 50 percent of global sales in the pet food, soups, breakfast cereals, and baby food categories. Much of this consolidation in market share was achieved through acquisitions, with many of the acquired companies continuing to operate under the original brand names[2].

Another structural factor impacting US jobs is the explosive growth of the global middle class (see Part Four). It is not unusual today to read about many of the US Fortune 500 companies that generate a substantial amount of their revenue outside the US. In addition to lower operating costs and 24/7 productivity opportunities, close proximity to and gaining market share in rapidly growing emerging markets, fewer tax and regulatory issues, global partnerships, supply chain advantages, and an export-focused strategy are explanations I frequently hear as reasons for this trend.

## Entrepreneurs & Disruptors: Competitive Advantages

Even the recipient countries of outsourcing can be disrupted. In recent business discussions I have had with clients and colleagues, companies continue to hire labor in locations with lower labor costs or supply chains closer to international markets. However, given some recent trends in these foreign markets, such as higher wages, inconsistent quality, increasing shipping costs, etc., companies are beginning to bring production back to their home countries. Yes, this is happening even here in the US. One way to bring jobs back to the US—or prevent them from going abroad in the first place— is to identify a competitive or cost-effective differentiator for the US-based job.

What competitive advantages can you and/or your business deliver? If you were a CEO, would you be willing to pay higher wages and taxes in the US to get any of the following:

Premium quality
Supply-chain advantages
Faster speed to market
Precision manufacturing
Outstanding customer service
Breakthrough innovation
Just-in-time inventory
R&D

## Mix & Match:

According to a recent Bureau of Labor Statistics (BLS) study on outsourcing, some of the most vulnerable job categories include those related to computer and administrative skills. Key questions used to determine job vulnerability to outsourcing included the degree to which

- Inputs/outputs can be transported cheaply or electronically
- Interaction with other employees is required
- Social or local knowledge is needed
- Duties are routine or can be handled by written instruction[3].

Which cost-effective differentiators can be applied to these categories? Which cost-effective differentiators can be applied to your own job category?

## Your Ideas:

# Issue 5:   Housing & Income Distribution

Sector:      Business & Finance

Location:    US


## Issue: Housing, the Income Distribution Gap & Poverty

The last two issues for your consideration are the impact of the housing industry and the growing income distribution gap affecting the US middle class—the consumer-spending engine that drives the economy.

For years, prior to the financial crisis and the subsequent recession, many Americans considered home ownership to be part of the American dream. Their homes would appreciate, helping to fund their lifestyles, their children's education, or their retirement. Suddenly, this came to a screeching halt. Leverage (remember those famous derivatives?) and risky mortgages drove certain financial institutions and housing-related companies out of business or into bankruptcy, dried up credit, caused a decline in new construction, and increased foreclosures, which helped drive down home values. For many, the dream burst. In the new normal, home ownership and consistent appreciation is not the funding source that it once was.

In 2006, prior to the recession, total US household equity was $13.5 trillion; at the end of 2009, it had fallen by over 60 percent to $5.3 trillion[1]. By 2013, with the gradual rebound of the housing industry some of these numbers are recovering. The housing crisis not only negatively affected household equity and consumer confidence, but it also affected employment. As one might expect, with the collapse in housing and the subsequent increase in foreclosures, many of these jobs directly and indirectly associated with the industry were negatively impacted. At the beginning of 2013, it appears that the housing industry is rebounding, and hopefully all of those jobs will return as well.

Another issue affecting consumer spending is the growing income distribution gap in the US. In 2011, the top 20 percent of US households represented 51 percent of adjusted income, and just the top 5 percent of households accounted for almost 22 percent of total adjusted income, while the bottom 20 percent of households accounted for a mere 3.3 percent[2]. The decades-long trend of eroding income in certain segments of the bottom 80 percent of the US population— along with increasing healthcare, energy, and educational expenses, and declining employment opportunities—has depressed consumer spending within those segments, and, thus, business revenues and profits in related industries and locations throughout the US.

This growing income gap has led to another factor impacting consumer spending: the growing poverty rate. In 2011, the US poverty rate was 15.7 percent and the number of Americans in poverty was a staggering 48.6 million, the largest number since estimates began more than fifty years ago[3]. Imagine what could happen to the US economy, businesses, entrepreneurship, innovation and job creation if we could move this enormous consumer segment out of poverty.

## Example: Renting

The positive counterbalance to declining home ownership is renting. Based on all of the new apartment construction and rate increases in my region, the rental model appears to be doing very well.

One entrepreneurial opportunity that has been created is the purchasing of some of the large supply of foreclosed or soon-to-be-foreclosed homes and turning them into rentals. With low mortgage rates and prices, an entrepreneur with a keen eye, the necessary skills and some cash might want to evaluate this sector.

## Entrepreneurs & Disruptors: Think Out of the Box

What segments of the housing industry represent out-of-the-box or non-traditional opportunities? Can any changes or variations be made to the following processes to create new business models?

Lending
Buying
Selling
Remodeling
Listing
Foreclosing
Construction
Interior decorating
Refinancing
Banking
Appraising
Landscaping

## Mix & Match:

Now, match your expertise or idea with the processes above and see what happens!

## Your Ideas:

# Summary:  Structural Shifts & Employment in the New Normal

It's a recession when your neighbor loses his job; it's a depression when you lose your own.

—President Harry S Truman

The eighteen-month recession from 2008–2009 and the prolonged, weak economic recovery were the result of both rampant financial speculation and the latest events in a gradual process of structural economic trends that the US economy has been experiencing for decades. These trends have created a new normal in employment and consumer spending. Whether we like it or not, the world is changing fast. Governments, institutions, organizations, and many companies are either unable or unwilling to adapt. With the 2012 presidential election over, we hope to see significant improvement in cooperation, leadership, problem-solving, investment, and job creation by both the public and private sectors. However, we can no longer depend on these traditional employers to provide all of our jobs. In the new normal, many individuals will have to consider creating their own jobs.

One solution for job creation is for voluntary and involuntary entrepreneurs to launch millions of new, innovative, micro-enterprises. These new engines of growth will help generate new jobs and help the US as it continues to maintain its global competitiveness, but this will require significant degrees of improvement in our commitment, infrastructure, and capabilities. This time, much of the effort will need to come from individuals like us—from the bottom up.

In Issues One through Five, several structural factors contributing to the new normal were highlighted, starting with the loss of high-paying manufacturing jobs. This is critical, since the manufacturing sector has traditionally been the base for high-paying middle-class jobs, which provide precious consumer spending to drive US and global economic recoveries.

One metric for understanding the new normal is the unemployment rate. However, the rate frequently reported by politicians and the media is not the whole story. To fully comprehend the impact of joblessness, we must include not just the BLS's U-3 measure, which includes total unemployed as a percent of the total labor force, but also the U-6 number, which includes "discouraged, marginally attached, and part-time workers"—the underemployed.

Another structural factor is that today many of the jobs that are being created come with lower pay and fewer benefits, while healthcare, education, and energy prices are increasing. We spent much of the last three decades financing our purchases by enjoying a credit binge that came to a screeching halt during the latest recession.

American workers have also been impacted by automation, off shoring, and industry consolidation. Technology and streamlined processes have increased productivity for companies, but they have also reduced the number of domestic jobs. The reality for American workers is that both automation and outsourcing have been going on for decades, and they will continue to do so. They are facilitated by rapidly evolving technology and the emergence and integration of large global markets.

The last issues discussed included the housing industry and the changing distribution of income in the US, which have impacted consumer confidence and spending, reducing business revenue and, consequently, hiring. Between 2006 and 2009, the total of US household equity had been more than cut in half. Regarding income distribution, since 1980, much of the income growth has been consolidated in the top 40 percent of households. In 2011, just the top 5 percent of households accounted for almost 22 percent of total adjusted income.

Now that we have considered some of the ongoing structural trends that contributed to the new normal in employment, let's look at some of the opportunities. The remainder of the book will briefly address the current entrepreneurial environment and present potential sector opportunities that will hopefully appeal to entrepreneurs, innovators, and disruptors both in the US and internationally.

# Part Two

HOW: ENTREPRENEURIAL "ENGINES OF GROWTH"—AGAIN

# Issue 6:   The Age of the Individual

Sector:     Culture & Society
Location:   Global


## Issue: You Are the Competitive Advantage

Our work is a significant element of our life and self-fulfillment.
During our lifetimes, we will most likely spend more time on work
than on any other activity. It affects our lifestyles, our attitudes,
the time we spend with friends and family, and how we feel about
ourselves. What we do for a living and how we do it is too important
to be left completely in the hands of others.

With the US U-3 unemployment rate stubbornly hovering just under
8 percent and the U-6 rate at around 14 percent, there are an estimated
22 million people unemployed, underemployed or marginally attached
to the labor force in the US (see Issue 2: on the Real Unemployment
Rate). Many of these individuals are facing long-term unemployment
with diminishing opportunities to obtain a job or salary comparable to
their last one. In this new normal, we can no longer just wait for others;
we must become more proactive. The good news is that this is a great
time for a motivated individual with a compelling idea, a solid business
plan, the right skills, support network, and some funding to consider
becoming an entrepreneur. One of the key factors for success is having a
competitive advantage—something that makes your business stand out
from the others. In the case of an individual—it's you!

You have one huge competitive advantage over everyone else: **yourself** and your perspectives.

Your environment, events, other people, your culture, religion, education, interests, and experiences have uniquely shaped you so that you can create innovative solutions to both common and complex problems. You are capable of inventing and/or potentially launching new products or improving current products and services to meet the ever-changing demands of the customer segments with which you are familiar. The way that you see opportunities around you is unique, so take the time to evaluate them.

Another competitive advantage is your deep knowledge of one or two very specific niche markets. Whether you are interested in things that are technical, scientific, demographic, medical, educational, international, traditional, or societal, or whether it involves leisure, food, entertainment, social media, hobbies, business, or sports, you can quickly and very inexpensively create your own website, blog, Facebook page, YouTube video, Twitter account, or mobile app (apps are not as easy as the others). The convergence of technology and media can help you jumpstart your entrepreneurial venture.

If you post a comment, send a tweet, update a page, or launch an app, you will quickly get feedback. There is no more waiting for focus groups or research; you can now test the market with prototypes, beta sites, flash sales, limited runs, daily deals, and production on demand. You can test marketing campaigns in hours and days, and you can learn, retool, and relaunch them to achieve greater return on investment (ROI). You can even present your idea as an open-source product and let the community build it with you.

## Opportunity: Tools for the Entrepreneurs

In addition to social and mobile media, quick access to relevant information, inexpensive software and hardware, low-cost space in the cloud, immediate and global access to potential customers, search engine optimization (SEO), and real-time, multi-channel communication and promotional capabilities are powerful tools that have become available to make the transition to the world of entrepreneurship possible. These tools, along with limitless information, reduce the barriers to self-employment. For example, three of my favorite magazines are *Fast Company, Wired and Inc.*. They are full of ideas, case studies, interviews and examples that will stimulate and inspire entrepreneurs and innovators. Information and technology are the great equalizers. They level the playing field, allowing individuals with skills and access to these tools to compete against the big players or in the global marketplace. You can now work from anywhere 24/7 with your mobile device as your virtual office.

## Example: Individuals, Internet, Impact

To completely understand the convergence of the power of an individual, an idea, and the appropriate technology, we simply need to remember the business models of the following companies:

| | |
|---|---|
| eBay | Wikipedia |
| Google | Yahoo |
| YouTube | MySpace |
| Amazon.com | Pinterest |
| iTunes | Craigslist |
| Skype | Facebook |
| Twitter | Pandora |
| Groupon | Zynga |
| LinkedIn | Tumblr |

Most of these companies were startups that were founded by one person or a small group of individuals with an idea. Some of their ideas disrupted entire industries, and several of these companies generated multibillion-dollar valuations. Some of these companies have fared better than others, but every day new candidates emerge and move up the food chain.

Let me remind everyone again that becoming an entrepreneur is neither easy nor is there a guarantee of success. According to the Census Bureau, depending on the industry, anywhere between 50–70% of new businesses fail within five years[1]. That is why I encourage aspiring entrepreneurs to either begin part-time or surround yourselves with experts that can help you navigate potential pitfalls and improve your odds of success.

## Entrepreneurs & Disruptors: In or Out of the Box?

As I stated before, the way that you see opportunities around you is unique. You may prefer traditional in-the-box solutions or you may take a more non-conformist, out-of-the-box approach. For example, take a look at some of the following jobs published by the University of California, San Diego Extension's annual report of the hottest jobs for college graduates[2]. It's noteworthy to see how many jobs revolve around systems, data, and computer networks.

Software & Web Developers
Physical Therapists
Market Research Analysts/Data Miners
Database Administrators
Information Security Analysts
Computer Network Architects & Systems Administrators

Think of both a traditional and non-traditional way to work in these areas and write them down in Your Ideas. Which ones appeal the most to you?

# Mix & Match:

Here are some options I thought about. Add your own categories.

| Area | In the Box | Out of the Box |
|------|-----------|----------------|
| Publishing | Traditional publisher | Self-publish an e-book. |
| Real Estate | Become an agent | Barter or home exchange |
| Medical | Open a retail clinic | Doctor makes house calls |
| Education | Become a teacher | Home school or internet tutor |
| Travel | Start a travel agency | Lead educational tours |
| Banking | Become a loan officer | Start a micro-loan program |
| Services | Collect recyclables | Design recycled products |

# Your Ideas:

# Issue 7: The Entrepreneurial Revolution

Sector:     Business & Finance
Location:   US & Global


## Issue: Thinking About Joining?

Either by choice or by necessity, growing masses of global entrepreneurs, innovators, and disruptors are emerging. Are you one of them? Are you a businessperson staring out of the airplane window, preparing your escape from your corporate job? Are you a frustrated technical expert whose mind is full of potential solutions waiting to be applied? Are you a recent graduate searching for an idea or committed to a life of being your own boss? Perhaps you are a member of the long-term unemployed or underemployed working part-time and you need to replace all or a portion of your lost income.

Maybe you are a returning war veteran (thank you for your service!) full of ideas and skills that can be turned into a successful business or an executive looking to balance work and family or a recent immigrant importing innovation from your home country or a farmer or artisan who wants to sell directly to customers around the world. Perhaps you are a small-business owner on the verge of unleashing disruptive commercial ideas that will revolutionize an out-of-synch business model, or maybe you are a single parent trying to make ends meet on rapidly diminishing resources. Are you a baby boomer who has both the idea and the capital to launch your own businesses? Has your retirement plan been altered, forcing you back to work, or are you a social entrepreneur whose idea could make a difference or change the world?

If you are an aspiring entrepreneur or innovator, perhaps the current economic and employment conditions have convinced you to consider taking the next step. Many people have asked me what the difference is between an innovator and an entrepreneur. In many cases, there is little if any difference, but based on my experiences, I have seen some patterns.

The innovator is the idea person, the inventor, the creative force, or the change agent. Frequently, the innovator has the idea but does not choose to or may not have the skills to turn the idea into a business. Enter the entrepreneur!

The entrepreneur is the businessperson, the risk-taker, the startup organizer, or the business-plan implementer. These are the people who may or may not have come up with the idea but enjoy turning an idea into a successful business. Despite the subtle distinctions between the two roles, they have many more similarities than differences.

Innovators and entrepreneurs are able to identify and evaluate opportunities from several perspectives, to rapidly identify potential markets and customers, to adapt quickly, to learn from failure, and to quickly re-launch. They are constantly looking for emerging trends, frustrated customers, unmet needs, or new products and services. They see things differently. Today, with access to current technology and information, you have the potential to join the entrepreneurial revolution.

## Opportunity: Information Overload

One of the most powerful tools for global entrepreneurs is access to critical information via multiple channels. Today with global internet penetration at 34%, 2.4 billion potential customers, advisors, collaborators, investors, mentors, partners, researchers, readers, shoppers, etc. around the world can access the web through multiple channels.[1]

Immediate access to unlimited information has many advantages, but it also has some disadvantages. One disadvantage is **information overload**, or too much information. How does your idea or business stand out in all the clutter and noise? What is relevant information? What is fact versus opinion? How do you find what you want? How do you connect with the right people? How can you be more efficient and not waste time searching for the information you want? Solving one of these problems or improving on a current solution can be a business model worth considering for certain segments of a 2.4 billion global Internet user market.

## Example: A Country of Small Businesses

In 2009, the Census Bureau listed 5.8 million employer firms (those with formal payrolls) operating in the US. Eighty-nine percent of these firms had fewer than twenty employees. They looked like this:

- 1–4 employees – 3.6 million firms – 62%
- 5–9 employees – 1.0 million firms – 17%
- 10–19 employees – 0.6 million firms – 10%

Although small entrepreneurial firms represent the vast majority of operating companies, they only account for 15 percent of total payroll. This honor goes to the firms with more than five hundred employees, which account for more than half of total US payroll[2].

## Entrepreneurs & Disruptors: Women Entrepreneurs & Decision-Makers

The role, influence, and impact of women entrepreneurs and small business owners in job creation in the new normal are critical. Based on my observations, business conversations, and consulting work, women appear to be a growing segment of small business owners, and they are networking and developing vast support groups. They are quickly establishing an environment and infrastructure to make it easier for women who have not felt comfortable entering into a business venture to launch their own business. According to the Small Business Administration, in 2008, the rate of self-employment for women was 7.1% compared to 9.8% overall. In 2007, women owned an estimated 29% of all non-farm businesses[3].

Women also control spending decisions. Globally, they control trillions of dollars in annual consumer spending. As I mentioned before, a key competitive advantage for an entrepreneur is the ability to identify potential markets and customers from varying perspectives. Many women are both the decision-makers and the customers who experience the complete relationship with a business. They can quickly understand whether businesses meet their expectations or not. If not, they can identify opportunities to provide something better.

## Mix & Match

List companies, products, or services you are familiar with that:

Provide poor customer service

Alienate their customers

Ignore certain types of customers because they are:

- Spending too little
- Unique
- Difficult to manage
- Unprofitable

Fail to meet changing customer demands

Charge too much for the value you receive

Now match these companies, products, or services with some of your solutions.

**Your Ideas:**

# Issue 8:   The Innovation/Usefulness Gap

Sector:     Science & Technology
Location:   US & Global

## Issue:  Connect the Dots

Many of today's innovative and technological discoveries are so
advanced, so complex and are communicated to society so quickly
that some of these breakthroughs quickly surpass the ability of the
average individual to either use or understand them. Technology
that is not well understood by the end-users may be seen as less
relevant or providing little, if any, usefulness to solve simple, day-to-
day problems—an innovation/usefulness gap. It is fertile ground for
innovative and entrepreneurial thinking.

On the other hand, some of these advancements can provide quantum
leaps in specific markets and customer segments. For example, the
computer, mobile devices, the Internet, solar-powered batteries,
electronics and medical technology have provided the world with
powerful solutions to help reduce poverty and improve healthcare,
education, energy self-sufficiency, and sustainable economic
development. One strategy for entrepreneurs is to match the simplest,
most cost-effective, and most easily applicable solution with a
compelling need. This matching process or connecting the dots is a
critical skill in identifying new or improved business opportunities.

# Opportunity: Oversized & Overpriced

The sophistication, scope, and global application of some current innovations are accelerating faster than the average individual may process or want to pay for. How many people do you know (I am one of them) who are tired of paying for product or service add-ons, unnecessary functionality, size, or quantity that they don't need, want, or understand? What if you have a simpler, cheaper, or more convenient product or service that was of a similar quality?

# Example: Less May Be More

Providing adequate product functionality or services at lower prices can be appealing to many customers. Discount retailers, brokers, airlines, fast food chains, and others have been doing this for decades. Given the lackluster economic recovery in the US and the long-term drain on consumer purchasing power, opportunities exist for entrepreneurs with streamlined business models to access over-served and under-served customer segments.

Think about the customer segments that are over-served or under-served by the following retail channels:

Luxury department stores
Mid-tier department stores
Discount stores
Dollar stores
Leasing businesses
Liquidators
Secondhand or consignment stores
Flea markets
Garage sales
Barter
Donations

## Entrepreneurs & Disruptors: Lower Price—Equal or Better Quality?

One of the key drivers for many consumers is price. What types of products or services can be offered at a lower price if you change one or more of the following features?

Size
Quantity
Shape
Production inputs
Production processes
Supply chain/logistics
Profit requirements
Packaging
Quality
Color
Point of sale
Customer support
Marketing/sales strategy

## Mix & Match

Now, combine the features you identified with your skill sets below.

Industry expertise

Functional expertise

Product expertise

Service expertise

Special talents and interests

## Your Ideas:

# Issue 9: The 1% Innovation & Entrepreneur Fund

Sector:     Culture & Society
Location:   US

## Issue: We Like Big Challenges (Besides, We May Not Have Much of a Choice)

Most businesspeople like goals, since they can be measured and they help to demonstrate progress. So, how about doubling the number of full-time and part-time startups in two years? It is a substantial challenge, but we are Americans and we think big, right? Before you sign up, let me put the target into context. It is not possible to quantify all of the startups in a given year, since many are part-time or never incorporated. Therefore it is difficult to have a comprehensive, baseline number but we could start with those that are incorporated or tracked in some way.

So where will these new incremental businesses come from? According to the BLS, in March of 2013, the size of the US civilian labor force was around 155 million people[1], and the seasonally adjusted U-6, which estimates the total unemployed, under-employed, and displaced workers (see Issue—The Real Unemployment Rate), was 13.9%. If I am not missing something, this represents over 20 million Americans who would like to have a full-time job but can't find one[2]. If just a small percentage of this group would launch even a part-time startup, we could make significant progress toward our goal.

# Opportunity: The 1% Innovation & Entrepreneur Fund

As previously stated, the failure rate for entrepreneurs is high, and failure happens for a wide variety of reasons, including poor business planning, inexperience, a lack of persistence, no access or limited access to capital, strong competition, and the lack of a market. Whatever the reason, having access to professional support and financial resources should improve the odds for success.

So what about a 1% Innovation & Entrepreneur Fund? Let's turbo-charge dormant or low-yielding capital. Interested individuals or organizations could voluntarily lend 1 percent of their discretionary money, and corporations could lend 1 percent of their $1.8 trillion of liquid assets[3] to the fund, turning a mountain of low-yielding capital into high-octane working capital. At the same time, 1 percent of corporate management teams, business professors, lawyers, accountants, and successful entrepreneurs could volunteer 1 percent of their time to mentor the startups. Relax—this has nothing to do with the redistribution of wealth or forced labor. It would be voluntary, and a local, state, or federal tax credit, an acceptable interest rate, or a small percentage of equity could be offered as an incentive for the loan. A respected, trusted, and experienced team of entrepreneurs for entrepreneurs could set up the guidelines and manage the fund. With the ability of startups to borrow from the fund and be supported by business experts, aspiring entrepreneurs could be encouraged to launch their own ventures. The benefits to participants and to the economy could be substantial.

By doubling new full-time and part-time businesses quickly over a concentrated period of time and providing the resources to improve their success rate, the resulting economic stimulus could provide a much-needed catalyst to catapult us out of this agonizing jobless recovery and enhance the current entrepreneurial infrastructure for the next wave of startups.

## The Global Super Rich & the "Multiplier Effect"

On a global basis, turning low interest-earning capital into smart working capital could have a stunning and positive effect on global economic development and employment. The recently released study *Estimating the Price of Offshore* has quantified that globally the 10 million richest individuals have deposited between $20 and 30 trillion—that's right, *trillion*—in private offshore banks. Only 100,000 of these people control close to $10 trillion, or an average of $100 million per individual[4]. According to the top fifty private banks, which manage an estimated $12 trillion of these funds, the deposits alone have had an average annual growth rate of 9 percent from 2005 to 2010[5]. The study estimates that instead of earning a 3 percent return, if those funds were taxed at a mutually acceptable rate by the home country (many are developing economies), they could generate large tax revenues that could significantly stimulate economic development and job creation[4].

Now, it is not the purpose of this book to debate the pros and cons of such a strategy, but I would like to highlight another approach that is periodically raised which is instead of simply taxing these individuals, incentivize them to put a percentage of their capital back to work in their home countries so that they can generate even more revenue for themselves, their businesses, and their communities. Smart investment is good business.

One thing I learned from my graduate work and my international business experience is the power of the multiplier effect from consumer spending. Simply put, the multiplier effect seeks to measure the cumulative impact of specific spending as it moves through an economy. Therefore, if some of those foreign deposits are invested in creating new businesses in the home economy, incremental jobs and salaries can be created, which then are used to buy products and services from others, who use those funds to do the same over and over again, multiplying the effect of the original spending and potentially benefiting the original business because of an increased level of consumer spending. If properly managed, these new businesses could be a win-win solution by providing greater overall returns to these wealthy individuals than their offshore accounts and generating faster and broader economic development for the country – just a thought.

## Example: US Entrepreneurs

What does the profile of current US entrepreneurs look like? According to the Kauffman Index of Entrepreneurial Activity, here are some characteristics:

- 6.3 percent of the adult population or 11.5 million people are self-employed business owners.
- Immigrants were more than twice as likely to start businesses.
- Arizona, Texas, California, Colorado, and Alaska had the highest rate of entrepreneurial activity.
- People between the ages of 20–34 years old, represented 29 percent of all new entrepreneurs.
- From 1996 to 2011, new entrepreneurs between 55–64 years old grew from 14 percent to 21 percent of the total[6].

## Entrepreneurs & Disruptors: Incubators, Accelerators, "Boot Camps," Co-Working Space, & Maybe Post Offices

In addition to a good idea, a strong business plan, and access to funding, many current and future startups need a place to network, share ideas, or just work. Over the last few years, several entrepreneurial models have been developed to stimulate and support the launch of small businesses. Regardless of the structure, most models provide the following services on a not-for-profit or for-profit basis:

- Free or subsidized rent, office and technology support
- Access to a network of industry, legal, financial, and marketing experts and mentors
- Access to funding sources or fund startups themselves
- Access to other startups

The most common model is the business incubator. Although it is difficult to get exact numbers because of the variations on the definition and locations, according to the National Business Incubator Association (NBIA) there are over one thousand incubators in North America. Over 90 percent of them are nonprofits, primarily local governments that are focused on job creation, and economic development organizations, or universities supporting the commercialization of their research and development. The others are for-profit incubators, which typically exchange services and funding for equity in the startups. Over two-thirds of the incubators operate in urban areas[7]

One problem for startups is the amount of time involved in the process itself, from concept development to business plan preparation to company formation to operations to proof of concept to funding and to hard launch. To shorten the cycle time and create more of a Darwinian approach to determine which startups survive and thrive, accelerators and boot camps have developed. As their names indicate, they are focused on improving the odds for success in a much shorter time.

Accelerators and boot camps rigorously screen applicants for the class and then put them through an intense and comprehensive process that lasts only a few weeks to a few months. Typically, these are for-profit models that exchange services and funding for equity in the graduating class. Recently, corporations have been getting involved in accelerators as a way to supplement their innovation strategy.

Finally, the most recent entrant into this category is the co-working space. Instead of camping out in a Starbucks or local Wi-Fi hotspots, younger entrepreneurs are getting free or low-cost temporary desk space in old houses, warehouses or lofts in urban centers. Here, they can network and collaborate with friends and colleagues to exchange or develop ideas, apps or new business models.

Currently, the press has been reporting that the US government continues evaluating the closure of thousands of post offices around the country, many of which are in rural areas. Typically, rural post offices have been one of the hubs of the community. In our goal to double the number of startups, what if local governments and entrepreneurs could work with the US Postal Service to reach a lease agreement to turn these valuable commercial hubs into local business incubators and co-working spaces? This model could provide economic development and job creation benefits (see Issue 20: Cities & Towns— Reinvent Yourselves), attract new incremental talent and businesses, retain young graduates, and even provide the economic support to keep the local post office running. In this new normal, we need to find creative solutions.

Nationally both formal and informal networks and infrastructure to support aspiring entrepreneurs, innovators, and disruptors already exist, and they continue to grow both locally and nationally. I am familiar with some organizations in the North Texas community that are doing a great job of that- Texchange, and Tech Wildcatters are just two examples and I participated in a Startup Weekend event which is an organization that is working both nationally and internationally (see Issue 23: Global Unemployment- Startup Weekend) — check them out!

# Mix & Match:

List your business ideas in column one, people you could potentially partner with in column two, and a local incubator, boot camp, or co-working space in column three.

**Ideas**             **Potential Partners**             **Local Organization**

# Your Ideas:

# Part Three

## WHAT: US ISSUES & TRENDS FOR ENTREPRENEURS & DISRUPTORS

Parts Three (US) and Four (International) focus on issues and markets that I believe represent current potential areas of opportunities for entrepreneurs and innovators. Part Three looks at macro trends and challenges that are relevant but not exclusive to the US. The irony with many of these issues is that they represent enormous potential opportunities, yet despite the huge demand for solutions and the abundance of talent, expertise, and money that already exist, they remain unresolved and they await new and innovative solutions on a grand or even micro-enterprise level. It's time!

# Issue 10:  High School Graduation Rates

Sector:      Education
Location:    US


## Issue: US Graduation Rate: 78%*

According to the most recent studies, the US public school system only graduates an estimated 78 percent of its students (as measured from their freshman year)[1]. Today's public school systems are confronted with multiple critical challenges that are waiting for solutions. One problem is low graduation rates, especially in large urban school districts. These low rates often lead to high unemployment, lower lifetime earnings potential, and other costs to the individuals and to society. Dropping out of school can trap bright and talented kids in a vicious cycle of poverty, and deprive our society of their contributions and innovation. Everyone deserves the right to an education and a lifetime of opportunity. We just need to design and implement the most effective models and expand those models that are already working well.

Graduation rates need significant improvement:

<u>**Graduation rate by ethnicity:**</u>

| | |
|---|---|
| African-Americans | 66% |
| Native Americans | 69% |
| Hispanic | 71% |
| White | 83% |
| Asian | 94%[2] |

*AFGR—average freshman graduation rate, 2008–2009

61

**Unemployment Rate by Education Level**

No high school diploma          12.7%
Diploma, no college             8.8%[3]

(February, 2013 – not seasonally adjusted)

Some general reasons for students dropping out include the following:

- 47% thought that the classes weren't interesting.
- 43% missed too much school and couldn't catch up.
- 38% had too much freedom and not enough rules.
- 35% were failing academically.
- 32% had to get a job and earn money[4].

A sizeable portion of the dropout challenge tends to be concentrated in a few school districts. Approximately 12 percent of US schools are responsible for almost half of all dropouts[5]. Consequently, a great dropout prevention program implemented in just a small number of schools could have a significantly positive impact on both graduation rates and the lives of thousands of students.

## Opportunity: Community Graduation Reactivation Program

Besides making classes more interesting, working with parents to ensure better attendance, and having at least one teacher or administrator who focuses on an individual student, what else can be done to help the 35 percent of dropouts who are failing academically? One solution for entrepreneurs to consider would be to develop a network of Community Graduation Reactivation Programs.

According to the US Dept. of Education, during the 2009-2010 school year, 514,000 public school students in grades 9-12 dropped out. This number does not include private school students[5]. This is unbelievable and unacceptable! At the same time, we are not retaining our teachers. In 2008–2009, 270,000 (8 percent) public school teachers and 77,000 (16 percent) private school teachers left teaching—347,000 teachers who were lost in just one year[6]. Again, this is unbelievable and unacceptable! This is where the Community Graduation Reactivation Program, or something similar, could become so effective.

What if we could re-hire or re-engage one-third of the most effective and motivated of those teachers on a full-time, part-time, or volunteer basis to teach as many of those dropouts as possible? How many students could we get to graduate if we had public and/or private micro-schools exclusively dedicated to dropouts of any age with a low student-teacher ratio and located in the heart of a community with a high dropout rate?

What about using church buildings as locations for some of these schools? This would be a great fit, since many churches already have unused classrooms during the week. Given the real-estate crisis in many communities, it should not be hard for a determined entrepreneur and a cooperative and innovative education department to find a clean, safe, and functional building to house a micro-school with free or subsidized rent, or rent sponsored by a business or an organization. If corporations, organizations or individuals can purchase naming rights to stadiums, fund endowments and college facilities, why not use the same process for community colleges, high schools, trade and vocational schools, specific departments, elementary schools, pre-school programs and even Community Graduation Reactivation Programs.


## Example: Learning Differences

Consider the 6–10 percent of the school-aged population in the US that have learning differences. Dyslexia, or the differences involved in a person's fluency or comprehension accuracy in being able to read, speak, and spell, is the most common condition. It is estimated that

10–17 percent or more of the population as a whole, may have some symptoms of dyslexia[7].

ADHD, or attention deficit hyperactivity disorder, is the most common behavioral issue in school-aged kids. According to the Center for Disease Control's 2011 Summary Health Statistics for US Children, an estimated 8 percent of children between the ages of three and seventeen are diagnosed with ADHD[8].

Students with either or both of these challenges have difficulty with traditional teaching methods, crowded and/or noisy classrooms and standardized testing, which requires strong mass memorization and test-taking skills. Low standardized test scores are not an adequate measure of these students' talents and capabilities, and these scores can result in students having low self-confidence and self-esteem which can also contribute to a desire to leave school.

Although programs and curricula exist to address these student segments, there is still a potential opportunity to develop even more accessible and effective national online or retail environments to provide these students with the tools that recognize their talents, support their educational development and confidence, and keep them in school.

## Entrepreneurs & Disruptors: The Right Skills for the Right Time

Education plays a critical role in economic development, individual success, and global competitiveness. Currently, certain segments of the US educational system are neither delivering the results we expect nor the number of graduates with skill sets required to drive the US economy in the new normal. Based on my conversations and media and business reporting, there seems to be a growing concern that the US is not producing enough high school graduates, graduates ready for freshman year, college graduates ready for the rapidly changing job market, or graduates who are globally competitive.

The US no longer ranks near the top internationally on key educational categories:

**US rank internationally:**

| | |
|---|---|
| Reading[1] | 14th |
| Math | 17th |
| Science | 25th[9] |

[1]Reading, math, and science ranks for fifteen-year-olds as assessed by the 2009 Programme for International Student Assessment

One common complaint from many businesses is that despite the high unemployment rate, many companies still cannot fill some open positions. They maintain that schools are not adequately preparing graduates with the skill sets needed by the businesses and the changing job market. Schools respond by saying they are hampered by lower tax revenue and budget cuts. More urgent public, private and entrepreneurial innovation is required to quickly resolve these issues. Businesses could provide more money and training in partnership with the educational community to become more actively involved in both the critical funding and retooling of key areas of the curricula and infrastructure. The demand is high and the necessary elements for solutions exist – we now need the commitment, leadership and innovation to quickly generate system-wide, tangible results.

## Mix & Match:

Randomly combine the categories below, or add your own items to the list (for example: game development + social studies = action games around key historical events).

| | |
|---|---|
| Graphic design | Game development |
| Music | Animation English/literature |
| Art | Science |
| Math | Social studies |
| Languages | Teaching |
| Tutoring | Subject matter expert |
| Mobile apps | Creative online lesson plans |
| Attendance | Alternative location/hours |

Now, evaluate the following concepts to see how you would apply them to these categories. Add others to these categories as well.

Gaming, music, and animation technology
Creative online lesson plans and teaching
Personalized, non-age-based curriculum
Reactivation of retired or frustrated teachers
Retention of best teachers
Private sponsorship of job skills training
Micro-schools with smaller classes
On-demand tutoring


**Your Ideas:**

# Issue 11:   The Baby Boomer Market

Sector:      Demographics & Markets
Location:    US

## Issue:  82 Million People

If you were born between 1946 and 1964, you are one of the baby boomers, the largest and most economically significant demographic segment of our lifetime. The 2010 US census estimated that 82 million people are in the boomer segment[1]. These savvy boomers represent both demand and supply-side markets for entrepreneurs.

### Demand

In 2011, thousands of baby boomers a day started turning sixty-five. This trend is estimated to continue until around 2030. Since the baby boomer segment accounts for an estimated 26 percent of the US population, it represents an important share of spending on a wide range of goods and services which is important for businesses of all sizes[2].

### Supply

Given the negative financial impact of the last recession on home equity, savings, pensions, 401(k)s, IRAs, and investment portfolios, many boomers have now become an unanticipated addition to the labor force, just as unemployment remains stubbornly high.

Many boomers don't have a choice. Their economic conditions will keep them working longer or force them to "retire from their retirement" and go back to work. They will either compete for existing jobs or create their own. Forty percent of boomers plan to work "until they drop"[3].

## Opportunity: Boom-trepreneurs

Given my interactions in the business community, discussions with clients and the negative impact that the recession had on boomer's financial and retirement plans, boomers are becoming a significant source of entrepreneurial activity, and they continue to develop innovative ideas to maintain their desires to stay active and improve their lifestyles and longevity. I believe linking these experienced business folks with younger app. developers, coders, web and graphic designers could generate a whole new set of micro-enterprises with a higher than normal success rate given the rich mix of operating experience and cutting-edge skill sets.

## Example: Healthcare

With access to more advanced healthcare, a focus on personal health, and a desire to have a better quality of life, many boomers will live longer and healthier lives, increasing their demand for new and redesigned products and services. This multibillion-dollar market is beginning to be addressed in areas such as:

- Anti-aging and preventive healthcare products
- Home healthcare services
- Quality-of-life medical products
- Life-long learning, computer training, new careers
- Volunteering, mentoring, teaching
- Residential communities with sporting and social activities
- Ergonomically designed products

- Educational, adventure, and medical tourism
- Personal services, such as shopping, transportation, cleaning, and senior housing

## Entrepreneurs & Disruptors: Segmentation

Identify a customer segment need and offer something unique, faster, simpler, cheaper, smaller, or more convenient. Try this simple exercise.

Pick a primary customer segment like retirees. Then pick a category like health. Potential customers can fall broadly into two sub-segments: healthy and unhealthy (or they can be categorized by age, gender, income, location, type of ailments, degree of wellness, access to healthcare and insurance, etc.). Then think about what each of these sub-segments need or will need.

| Segment | Category | Sub-segment | Opportunity | Business |
|---------|----------|-------------|-------------|----------|
| Retirees | Health | Unhealthy | Affordable home care | Lower-cost, services |
| | | Healthy | Preventive healthcare | Lower-cost, self-diagnostic devices |

## Mix & Match:

Try the same exercise with your own primary segments and categories.

## Your Ideas:

# Issue 12:   Extreme Weather

Sector:         The Environment
Location:      US & Global

## Issue: Sweating Yet?

The planet is warming. The endless and heated debate over the causes
of global warming has resulted in a paralysis of action from many
of the key players, which does not appear likely to be resolved soon.
Entrepreneurs and innovators aren't waiting around. They are attacking
the problem. When you are standing in a fire, you get out—you don't
stay in the fire debating how the fire got started or who started it.
Entrepreneurs, innovators, and certain businesses are testing and
applying solutions, and they are addressing key issues, but there is
much more that needs to be done.

If you think it has been hotter recently, you're right. Between June
2011 and June 2012, the US experienced the warmest twelve-month
period since record-keeping began in 1895[1]. The previous decade was
no different. According to the National Oceanic and Atmospheric
Administration (NOAA), not including the last twelve months, the ten
warmest average temperatures recorded globally since 1880 happened
within the last thirteen years.

| Rank | Year |
|------|------|
| 1 & 2 | 2005 & 2010 |
| 3 | 1998 |
| 4 & 5 | 2003 & 2002 |
| 6 & 7 | 2006 & 2009 |
| 8 | 2007 |
| 9 | 2004 |
| 10 | 2001 |
| 11 & 12 | 2008 & 1997 |
| 13 | 1999 |
| 14 | 1995 |
| 15 | 2000[2] |

This global warming trend coincides with spectacular displays of Mother Nature's extreme weather. Examples of extreme weather are becoming more and more frequent. Just a week before the 2012 presidential election, the perfect storm, Hurricane Sandy, devastated parts of the Northeast coast and flooded low-lying areas of New Jersey and New York City. There is already discussion on what can be done to prevent or reduce damage from similar future storms.

## Opportunity: Extreme Ideas

Opportunities, solutions, adaptations, and enhancements in extreme situations can sometimes be easier to identify because they are glaringly obvious. Think about what will be needed when people are faced with more frequent and extreme changes in temperature, rainfall, sea levels, storm intensity, water management, food production, and the spread of disease.

- Longer-term weather forecasting services at less cost
- Products or services for areas impacted by droughts or floods
- New water-management, flood control, and design ideas
- Storm management and cleanup

- Storm-resistant and green construction
- Low-cost, off-the-grid mini-heaters, generators and air conditioners for temporary and perhaps life-saving relief from extreme temperatures
- Early disease-detection and quarantine processes

## Example: Agricultural Hotspots, Food Insecurity, and Production

According to the report "*Mapping Hotspots of Climate Change and Food Insecurity in the Global Tropics*" persistent climate change could negatively impact food production and supply in select parts of the world. Those most affected could include certain areas of South Asia and India, Sub-Saharan, eastern, and southern Africa, China, Northeastern Brazil, and Mexico. Crops such as beans and corn could be diminished by higher temperatures or shorter growing seasons[3].

Innovative solutions will be needed to prevent critical food shortages when such scenarios become reality. However, if local solutions are insufficient to meet demand then one solution might be increased production from farmers in the northern Great Plains, Canada, Europe, Brazil, and Argentina, who may benefit from longer and more moderate growing seasons. If this happens then access to global markets, distribution, and logistics—extraordinarily expensive and complicated processes—represents a large potential opportunity. There is, however, just one problem: what if these regions are simultaneously affected as well? As I write this book, the media is full of stories regarding the widespread drought in the US and the impact it will have on US agricultural production, world food supplies, and prices.

# Entrepreneurs & Disruptors: Tornadoes, Floods, & Hurricanes—Oh, My!

The effects of extreme weather can be both emotional and economic, as portrayed by frequent media coverage of these tragic events. For individuals, a severe storm and its aftermath or extreme temperatures can be life-threatening and/or psychologically stressful. For businesses or industries dependent on weather, the effects can be financially devastating. Products or services that can help mitigate such risks represent potentially significant market niches.

## Mix & Match:

Compare your state to another state with weather patterns that are the opposite. Now match those states with some of the categories listed in the Opportunity section. For example, what agricultural opportunities can you identify in the following categories?

Drainage and irrigation

Drought-resistant crops

Less-expensive pest control

Longer growing seasons in traditionally cooler climates

Geo-targeted soil-management information and products

Changing biodiversity and crop rotation patterns

Genetically modified seeds

Rapidly changing food supply, demand, pricing, and supply-chain issues

Livestock management

## Your Ideas:

# Issue 13:   Habla Español?

Sector:        Demographics & Markets
Location:    US

## Issue: Un Mercado Importante

The 2010 census indicated that 16 percent of the US population was of Hispanic or Latino origin. This segment of the population is growing quickly and accounts for over half of the total US population increase over the last ten years[1]. It appears that this trend will continue for decades. The Census Bureau projects that the Hispanic population will double by 2060 and represent around a third of the US population[2]. One powerful tool for entrepreneurs is to understand and use demographic data and trends to identify growing market segments. Like baby boomers, the various Hispanic and Latino segments will be significant over the next several decades. One clear example of their influence was seen in the political power they leveraged in key local and federal races during the 2012 presidential election.

The majority of Hispanics live in the largest states and more than half live in just three states: California, Texas, and Florida. If you add five others—New York, Illinois, Arizona, New Jersey, and Colorado—you account for 75 percent of the Hispanic population in 2010[1].

## Top cities with majority Hispanic populations

| | |
|---|---|
| East Los Angeles, CA | 97% |
| Laredo, TX | 96% |
| Hialeah, FL | 95% |
| Brownsville, TX | 93% |
| McAllen, TX | 85% |
| El Paso, TX | 81%[1] |

The two states with the fastest-growing Hispanic population growth rates during the last decade were South Carolina, which grew 148 percent, and Alabama, with a growth rate of 145 percent[3].

One key to working with demographic segments is to divide them into sub-segments to gain a greater awareness and a deeper understanding of the micro-trends or characteristics in each group. For example, look at the country of family origin, the language preferences, the cultural attributes, the generational differences, the consumption habits, and the preferences of a given demographic segment to learn much more.

# Opportunity: De Dónde Eres?

If we sub-segment the US Hispanic population by country of family origin for the largest five groups, we discover the following:

| % age of Hispanics | | Pop. (millions) | % chg, 2000–10 |
|---|---|---|---|
| Total | 100.0% | 50.5 | 43% |
| Mexican | 63.0 | 31.8 | 54 |
| Puerto Rican | 9.2 | 4.6 | 36 |
| Cuban | 3.5 | 1.8 | 44 |
| Salvadoran | 3.3 | 1.6 | 152 |
| Dominican | 2.8 | 1.4 | 85 |
| Top 5 | 81.8% | 41.3[1] | |

One interesting observation is that almost two-thirds of the US Hispanic or Latino population originated from Mexico, while the fastest-growing segment is Salvadoran, which has grown 152 percent since 2000.

## Example: Dónde Vive Usted?

If we further sub-segment these groups by the top five states with the largest population by family origin, we find the following ranking:

| | | | | | |
|---|---|---|---|---|---|
| Mexican | CA | TX | AZ | IL | CO |
| Puerto Rican | NY | FL | NJ | PA | MA |
| Cuban | FL | CA | NJ | NY | TX |
| Salvadoran | CA | TX | NY | VA | MD |
| Dominican | NY | NJ | FL | MA | PA[1] |

## Entrepreneurs & Disruptors: Nostalgia, Imports, & Exports

Having worked and lived in Latin America, and having many Hispanic friends and family members, I frequently hear about the desire for products and services to provide a link or connection to their country of family origin. This nostalgic desire to stay connected to family, friends, and their cultural heritage is especially strong for first-generation and second-generation families. Whether it is a particular food, beverage, song, magazine, newspaper, TV show, sports team, type of clothing, or political event, these links are significant opportunities for entrepreneurs.

A couple of years ago, as part of an international business exchange program sponsored by the World Affairs Council of Dallas/Fort Worth and the U.S. State Dept., I spent two weeks in Peru with Peruvian entrepreneurs as a follow-up to their trip to the US to meet and spend time with their business counterparts. The trip confirmed what I had observed for decades: there are brilliant and talented entrepreneurs and innovators everywhere in the world, and ideas and business models can originate on both sides of the border. Ideas, as well as products, can be both imported or exported.

Although it is not easy to navigate the regulations and logistics of the import/export business, it can be done, and the opportunities to access a much larger and more diverse market are generally worth the effort. The US government and private firms are great resources that can provide training, certification, and even turnkey processes and infrastructure to help you get started.

## Mix & Match:

Answer the following questions and see if you can generate a business opportunity or two.

What language(s) do you speak?

Do you have family or friends with Hispanic backgrounds?

Do you have family or friends who live in a Spanish-speaking country?

What are the countries that you are the most familiar with?

What industry do you know well?

What are your top three skill sets?

Have you ever imported or exported products?

In what products or services are you most interested?

What are two of your unique talents or interests?

# Your Ideas:

# Issue 14:   Disruptive Innovation

Sector:      Science & Technology
Location:    US

## Issue: Keep Looking Over Your Shoulder

In his fascinating book, *The Innovator's Dilemma: When New Technologies Cause Great Firms to Fail,* Harvard professor Clayton Christensen describes how some companies develop goods or services that are too expensive or too advanced for some of their customers which can create customer dissatisfaction or demand for other products or services. Clever competitors and innovators can begin to serve these dissatisfied customers by offering cheaper or less sophisticated products or services. Eventually, some of these innovators grow large enough to become significant competitors and some may even disrupt an industry[1].

As a former corporate executive and a current entrepreneur and investor, I have seen both sides of this concept. Although it's more difficult, I find the disruptor role to be exciting and more suited to entrepreneurs rather than large companies. I must admit, however, that innovation does not always fit neatly into one of these categories. Just doing something cheaper, or more efficiently than your competition does not automatically make you a disruptor. It just makes you more competitive and perhaps more successful—which is just fine.

I believe we will see an explosion of disruptive innovation in the new normal due to a convergence of two key factors. First, on the demand side, the structural nature of the economic downturn and higher costs have reduced buying power in certain consumer segments and forced many consumers, and even some businesses, to seek out lower-cost options (see Issue 16: The Age of Thrift), which they may continue to do for years to come. Less-expensive but basic, quality products and services with fewer bells and whistles will become more acceptable and possibly even more desirable.

Second, on the labor supply side, to generate higher productivity ratios and to protect profitability, companies continue to cut costs, reduce research and development, and become more risk-averse. Many experts have been laid off or have taken buy-out or early retirement packages in what continues to be a critical brain drain for US companies. When these experts leave the company, their expertise and valuable knowledge of their industry, former products, services, and customers' needs leave with them. Out of necessity, some will become involuntary entrepreneurs, and some will become formidable competitors or major disruptors to their former employers.

## Opportunity: I Am Never Shopping Here Again!

To become a successful entrepreneur, you don't have to have the idea itself to disrupt an industry, or even a large multinational corporation, but you should have a model with a legitimate competitive differentiator that can be profitably and consistently executed. Whether you are a disruptor or an entrepreneur, identifying a vulnerable business model or industry will be key. Look for companies, products, or services that:

- Provide poor customer service (not hard to find)
- Alienate their customers (not difficult to find either)
- Ignore customers because they are too:
    Small of a segment
    Difficult to manage

> Hard to find
> Unprofitable or not profitable enough

- Fail to meet changing customer demands
- Do not operate their businesses efficiently
- Charge too much for the value that is received
- Provide inferior quality products or services
- Force you to pay for stuff you don't want (a particular pet peeve of mine)

These businesses are everywhere and, based on my own and my family's experiences as consumers, and my consulting, the number of these businesses is increasing. You spend your hard-earned money with them all the time. They include local restaurants, lawn services, auto mechanics, medical practices, regional supermarkets, service providers, energy companies, educational institutions, retailers and national telephone, insurance, software, and airline companies. Many of these businesses and brands are vulnerable to losing market share or even being replaced by a better, more customer-focused business model.

## Example: Disruption in Progress

One way that companies cut costs during the economic downturn is to reduce business travel by using videoconferencing. Rather than putting people on the road, they put them in conference rooms with cameras, screens, speakers, and software to communicate with colleagues or business contacts anywhere in the world.

One of the pioneers in videoconferencing was Skype, which opened up visual communication to virtually anyone with a PC and camera. Originally, the quality and connectivity were inconsistent, but it was still free. Eventually other innovators entered the market with a variety of competitive products and services.

Videoconferencing has not completely disrupted business travel, but it is having an impact. Today, the competition is on to offer less-expensive options to larger market segments through alternative distribution channels, which rent the technology by the day or by the hour. This is an interesting space to keep your eye on.

## Entrepreneurs & Disruptors: Seize the Moment

If you plan on competing with or disrupting an existing business model, doing so in the new normal may be a good time. Some companies may be distracted or in a holding pattern waiting for the economy to bounce back. Entrepreneurs and disruptors have a distinct advantage over many businesses because they are accustomed to change and they are quicker to identify emerging opportunities, frustrated customers, unmet needs, new products, and national and international opportunities.

If you don't want to launch your idea yourself but you simply want to license or sell it, this may also be a good time to do so. During a slow economy, companies look for lower-cost, innovative solutions. Just look at the amount of start-ups acquired or recent M&A activity in your community as a good indicator. Your idea could be just what they are looking for. Make sure to get professional legal and financial advice before agreeing to the terms of any contract. Remember:

- Concentrate on one clear idea.
- Focus like a laser beam on your targeted customer segment.
- Keep it simple and easy for consumers to understand.

## Mix & Match:

Once you have found a new or vulnerable business model, what type of competitive differentiator or disruptor can you identify?

Different size
Less expensive
Simpler to understand or use
Different shape
Unique production inputs
Better management expertise
Production processes
Supply chain/logistical advantage
Better packaging
More efficient operations
Less quality for a lower price
Unique color
More points of sale
Better customer support
More effective marketing/sales strategy


## Your Ideas:

# Issue 15:   Healthcare: New Ideas Needed—Stat

Sector:        Health

Location:     US

## Issue: This Makes My Head Hurt

One sector that is very vulnerable to disruption and is in need of new
ideas is healthcare. In the new normal, stubbornly high unemployment,
reductions in healthcare benefits offered by employers, and exploding
insurance premiums for less coverage have resulted in a staggering
number of the US population going without health insurance coverage
and subsequently delaying or not seeking necessary nor preventive
healthcare. In 2011, it was estimated that over 48 million people,
or 15.7 percent of the entire US population, went without health
insurance[1].

In 2010, the government passed a healthcare reform law called the
Affordable Care Act, which was upheld by the US Supreme Court in
mid-2012[2]. With the 2012 presidential election completed, the impact
of Obamacare on the uninsured and on healthcare delivery remains to
be seen. The bottom line is that the inability of millions of Americans
to afford or access adequate healthcare is a significant issue that
requires new ideas and models to provide solutions.

## Opportunity: The Uninsured

We can again use Census Bureau data to learn more about the various characteristics of the uninsured and to identify the segments that may have the greatest healthcare challenges.

| Segments | Characteristics | % Uninsured |
| --- | --- | --- |
| US Population | Uninsured | 16.3 |
| Origin | Hispanic | 30.7 |
| Age | 18–24 | 27.2 |
| | 25–34 | 28.4 |
| Work Experience | Less than full-time | 28.5 |
| HH Income | Less than $25,000 | 26.9 |
| Region | Southern US | 19.1 |
| Residence | Inside major cities | 19.4[3] |

So, generally speaking, younger, lower-income adults who live in large cities and are not working full-time have the greatest likelihood of not having health insurance.

## Example: The 48/5 Principle

In the US in 2009, we spent an estimated $7,960 per person, on healthcare[4]. This is almost double the amount per person we spent in 1997. For an entrepreneur with a healthcare idea, it is important to understand that a significant amount of healthcare spending is concentrated among a small portion of individuals with serious or chronic conditions, as shown below.

| % US pop. by healthcare $ | | % $ spent on healthcare | $ spent/ person |
| --- | --- | --- | --- |
| Bottom | 50% | 3% | $    233 |
| Top | 5% | 48% | $35,829 |
| Top | 1% | 22% | $90,061[5] |

What a range! Fifty percent of the population accounts for a mere 3 percent of healthcare spending, while the top 5 percent (those with the most serious and/or chronic conditions) account for almost half of healthcare spending. Be careful and don't assume that some portion of the 50 percent didn't need healthcare just because they did not show expenditures. Some of them accessed free medical care, while many others may have delayed seeking treatment. This is especially important for those with chronic health conditions, where low-cost preventive care could delay or prevent their moving into the high-spending category with serious untreated conditions. The old adage "either you pay now or you pay later" seems to be true in healthcare.

## Entrepreneurs & Disruptors: Chronic Conditions & Age

What else can we learn about these groups, and how they might provide opportunities for new entrepreneurial ideas? First, we can identify the most-expensive health conditions, which are heart disease, cancer, trauma, mental disorders, and pulmonary issues[5]. Unfortunately, most of us either personally or through a friend or family member have had experience with one or more of these conditions. Although the expertise, technology, and medications today are outstanding and improving, they are also very costly.

As one would expect, age is also a factor in healthcare spending. Of the bottom 50 percent who spend only 3 percent on healthcare, 64 percent are thirty-four years old or younger, while in the top 5 percent of spenders, 42 percent of the individuals are sixty-five years old or older[6]. Big potential opportunities exist for entrepreneurs and disruptors who can develop businesses to address the unmet needs of healthcare providers or patients in this top 5 percent category.

## Mix & Match:

Are you a physician, nurse or other type of care provider?

What are your specialties?

Do you work in the health insurance industry?

What opportunities exist to lower costs or to become more efficient?

What process improvements can be made in medical record-keeping and record accuracy?

What opportunities exist with electronic medical records technology?

What innovative types of retail locations could be used to reach the uninsured?

What new processes can be implemented to improve or accelerate R&D?


## Your Ideas:

# Issue 16:   The Age of Thrift

Sector:        Culture & Society
Location:      US


## Issue: Got Groupons?

As I have mentioned frequently throughout the book, one of the
structural trends in the employment new normal we are experiencing is
the gradual decline in certain Americans' buying power, which plays a
key role in the US economy. This decline has been impacted by higher
unemployment, lower-paying jobs, and reduced availability and use
of credit. One result of this phenomenon is the need to become more
frugal. When you have fewer dollars, those dollars need to provide
greater value.

When budgets are reduced, individuals and households prioritize
what they can afford; they identify what they must cut, and they
figure out how to make their money go farther—a good exercise for
politicians and governments. Although housing, food, critical medical
care, transportation to work, etc. are generally priorities, in an age of
thrift they can be replaced by less-expensive substitutes like renting
instead of owning a home, shopping at discount stores, going to free
clinics, and using public transportation. Other discretionary purchases
may be delayed or eliminated, such as entertainment, vacations, new
purchases, and home improvements, which highlights the precarious
downward spiral that exists in some industries. Declining income leads
to declining buying power, which leads to lower business revenue and
profits, which lead to less hiring, which leads to less consumer income.

Reduced spending is not limited to just products. The latest recession generated a 7 percent decline in discretionary spending on services like recreation, transportation, food service, and utilities, which was double the next largest decline, which occurred in the early '80s[1]. Although this aspect of the new normal is becoming increasingly more difficult for many American consumers and the companies that rely upon them, for entrepreneurs this shift in consumer behavior presents an opportunity to adapt current business models or to start new ones to meet the shift in demand.

## Opportunity: Where Can I Get a Good Deal?

The purchasing behavior of certain consumer segments in this Age of Thrift is changing, and it is ushering in opportunities for entrepreneurs to both identify and respond to these changes. Here are a few changes that I have noticed with family, friends, and clients:

1. **Researching**—With less available money, consumers are less comfortable taking a chance on a purchase that does not meet their requirements or expectations. Internet reviews and word-of-mouth recommendations are two reliable channels for consumer information and advertising. Social media and websites that post reviews are really supporting this trend.

2. **Power couponing and cash back**—From the viewpoint of many consumer's, buying the products and services they like and trust at a reduced price is easier than substituting these products for other brands. From the retailer's point of view, the strategy to provide discounts to attract new consumers, to gain market share, to motivate customers to try other products or services, or to shop during off-hours is growing, as are the distribution channels for offering these discounts. Groupon, Living Social, and other companies were initially very effective in using both the web and mobile devices to provide consumers

with significant discounts. Recently however, these models have fallen back from their peak performance. The retailers accepting these daily deals need to be careful, however, to ensure that the coupon, cash back, or discount strategy that they are using is either profitable for them or supports their overall business strategies.

3.  **Buying less**—I think that this is a good opportunity for disruption. More and more, I am noticing that products are packaged, bundled, and made larger than they should be as a way of forcing me to buy stuff that I don't need and for which I certainly don't want to pay extra. Consider renting which may be better than buying, and renting by the hour may be better than renting by the day. Unbundle the package - think smaller, and cheaper!

4.  **Delaying purchasing**—Individuals are stretching their dollars by delaying visits to the hairdresser, the doctor, the auto dealer, the financial planner, the mall, the restaurant, the movies, or by scheduling plumbers, electricians, and landscapers less often. What entrepreneurial models could be launched to address the needs of this change in consumer behavior?

## Example: Dollar stores

As one might expect, over the last few years the growth of dollar stores has exploded. Companies like Dollar General, Family Dollar Stores, and Dollar Tree have opened hundreds of new stores that offer thousands of low-cost products (see Issue 8: Example—Less May Be More). In 2009, 53 percent of consumers, which included many middle-class and affluent consumers, shopped at a dollar store[2]. With a network of thousands of stores and growing, these businesses are not only competing with other low-priced retailers; they have also now begun to compete with local grocery and drugstores.

## Entrepreneurs & Disruptors: How Much of Your Stuff Do You *Really* Use?

Understanding shifts in consumer behavior and building a business to address one or more of these shifts should be a core competency of entrepreneurs, innovators, and disruptors. One fascinating segment is the sale or rental of recycled or used products. This concept represents the convergence of several trends. Reusing perfectly fine items is becoming more acceptable for consumers interested in thrift, value, green, sustainable, and vintage products. These products range from clothing and clothing accessories to equipment, vehicles, electronics, furniture, household items, books, art, movies, games, etc.

Gently used, pre-owned, antique, re-purposed, or vintage products sold online or in retail stores, flea markets, garage sales, on consignment, in cooperatives, charitable donation stores, or pawnshops tend to be in greater supply and demand during economic downturns. When times are good and credit is available, we tend to buy lots of stuff, much of which we seldom use. For example, what percent of the clothes and shoes in your closet do you wear? How much of the stuff in your garage or in storage do you use? I personally only use maybe 30 percent of the stuff that is in my garage or closet. A couple of interesting business models would be to offer these items for sale or trade, or to broker transactions between buyers and sellers, especially if you have a distinct market niche.

## Mix & Match:

What skills or business ideas do you have for:

Helping frugalistas find or research money-saving strategies or products?

Helping retailers and merchants develop profitable couponing, cash back, or discounting strategies?

Developing simpler, smaller, cheaper products or services to compete against vulnerable business models?

Providing bridge products or services to meet customer needs while they delay purchases?

Matching buyers and sellers of recycled products?


## Your Ideas:

# Issue 17:   Local Food

Sector:         Demographics & Markets
Location:       US


## Issue: So, This Broccoli Comes from Where?

It is becoming increasingly popular to grow, sell, and consume food
locally instead of shipping it across the country or importing it. Led
by environmentalists, local and organic farmers, health-conscious
consumers, grocers, retailers, chefs, caterers, and community tourism
groups, the local food movement represents a growing opportunity for
entrepreneurs. According to USDA's Agricultural Marketing Service,
from 1998 to 2009 the number of farmers' markets in the US increased
90% to 5,274[1].

Although this sector is growing, there appears to be no clear
definition of a "local food product." The 2008 Food, Conservation,
and Energy Act uses a metric that states that local food products
must be "transported less than four hundred miles from its origin, or
within the state in which it is produced." In addition to growing the
food, typically, these local producers do a bit of everything, including
marketing, storing, packaging, transporting, distributing, and supply
chain functions. These producers who sell directly to consumers are
typically small, and they are generally located near urban centers, close
to their consumer base[1].

Advocates maintain that local food solves several problems. It decreases
the cost and the carbon footprint by reducing food miles. It provides

food that is fresher and higher in nutrients. There is less spoilage, producers earn more by selling direct to consumers, and communities benefit through more local spending.

Ironically, while the local food movement is growing, importing certain types of food into the US is also increasing. According to the Department of Agriculture, between 1999 and 2011, the total value of US food imports has increased by 160%. Some of the key categories can be seen in the chart below.

<u>**Value of US Food Imports**</u> (1999–2011)

| Key categories | % age increase from 1999 |
|---|---|
| Vegetable oil | 340% |
| Cereals & bakery | 240 |
| Sugar & candy | 201 |
| Vegetables | 170 |
| Fruits | 162 |
| Nuts | 152 |
| Coffee & tea | 143[2] |

Some large grocers, retailers and restaurants are starting to increase their purchases of locally grown produce (although definitions of "locally grown produce" are quite broad), which is good news for individuals either currently working or contemplating working in this sector.

## Opportunity: CO-OPeration

For some people, getting into the local food movement may require assistance, since some of the steps can be more complicated than they appear to be. This demand for training and/or broadening of skills provides opportunities for entrepreneurs to assist current or aspiring food producers in:

- Expanding producer capacity, quality & productivity
- Utilizing new equipment or expanding irrigation systems
- Improving distribution systems
- Negotiating contracts
- Marketing directly to consumers
- Regulatory compliance[1].

# Example: Gardening

Gardening continues to be popular due to various factors, including a desire for fresh-tasting produce and healthier fruits and vegetables, an enjoyment of gardening, and a prolonged economic downturn motivating more people to grow their own favorite foods. The National Gardening Association indicated that 43 million US households intended to grow their own produce in 2009, up 19 percent from pre-recession 2008[3].

**Community & Urban Farming**

There are an estimated eighteen thousand community gardens throughout the United States and Canada[3]. These are gardens that are planted and managed by the community and that provide many benefits, including the following:

- Feeding local people
- Improving local air quality & environment
- Providing job training
- Keeping people physically fit
- Teaching green practices

## Entrepreneurs & Disruptors: Think Process!

If you think about the potential product opportunities in this sector, you should also think about the process. For example, a beginning gardener may need how-to information, a space for a garden, tools, clothing, seeds or plants, organic or chemical treatment for fertilizing, insects or diseases, and information about harvesting, storage or marketing

## Mix & Match:

Do you have an idea for a gardening product or service or the local food movement that involves any of the following?

Information or inventions

Unique spaces for a garden

Tools

Clothing and accessories

Seeds

Plants

Organic treatment for fertilizing and dealing with insects and diseases

Fencing

Canning and storing food

Recipes

Nutritional tips

Other

# Your Ideas:

# Issue 18:   Web & Mobile Business

Sector:       Business & Finance
Location:     US


## Issue: There's an App for That

Like many other people, I believe that the single most-powerful tool for providing the foundation for the global entrepreneurial revolution has been and continues to be the Internet. Today, with the explosion of mobile device usage and hundreds of thousands of apps, individuals from around the world can quickly see and respond to your product, service, blog, video, or tweet. This is both good and bad news. With greater access to customers also come issues of privacy, data security and monitoring comments about you and your business in a 24/7 world. Again this presents both challenges and possible opportunities for entrepreneurs and disruptors.

Expanded communication and e-commerce channels now make it easier to launch your web-based or mobile-based business with limited funds and experience. Today, for a few hundred dollars, you can launch and host an off-the-shelf template website to advertise and communicate your business. For a few thousand dollars more, you can add an e-commerce capability or mobile app to actually buy and sell, and conduct payment transactions. Even more easily, you can sell your products or services on someone else's website and piggyback off of their e-commerce platform, further reducing your cost and barriers to entry.

In mid 2012, global Internet usage reached over 2.4 billion people, representing 34 percent penetration worldwide (see Issue 7: Opportunity—Information Overload). The ability for entrepreneurs and innovators to reach these individuals is becoming easier. Asia has the largest number of Internet users, but North America has close to 80 percent penetration.

**Global Internet Usage** (Q2, 2012):

| Internet (millions) | Users | Penetration (%) |
|---|---|---|
| North America | 273 | 79 |
| Australia/Oceania | 24 | 68 |
| Europe | 518 | 64 |
| Latin America | 255 | 43 |
| Middle East | 90 | 40 |
| Asia | 1,077 | 28 |
| Africa | 167 | 16 |
| Total | 2,406 | 34%[1] |

Many well-known US websites represent examples of the business infrastructure and support available to entrepreneurs: information, search, R&D, networking, communication, collaboration, advertising, funding, buying and selling globally—everything is at your fingertips.

**Top 10 US Websites**

1. Google
2. Facebook
3. YouTube
4. Yahoo!
5. Amazon.com
6. eBay
7. Craigslist.org
8. Wikipedia
9. Twitter
10. Windows Live[2]

# Opportunity: "Mobile World"

**"By 2016, there will be more than eight billion handheld or personal mobile-ready devices and nearly two billion machine-to-machine connections."**

Press Release: Cisco® Visual Networking Index (VNI) Global Mobile Data Traffic Forecast for 2011 to 2016

Having spent most of my career in business, I believe that the optimal situation for a potential sale is putting the right offer in front of the right customer at exactly the right time. Putting the right offer in front of the right customer is as much an art as it is a science, and it still appears difficult for many businesses to master. Some examples of the wrong offer reaching the wrong people include when your ten-year-old child or your dog receives a credit card application, or your ninety-year-old grandmother receives her daily deal coupon offer for a discount on a mountain bike or Zumba classes (See Issue 21: Customer Relationship Management, CRM).

However, if you can get the offer and the customer right then you might have a competitive advantage in using a mobile app to put those offers in front of customers when they are ready to buy. This is a powerful combination that can either be really successful or, in the case of an unprofitable incentive offered to hundreds or thousands of redeemers, it can be disastrous. Run your numbers beforehand and make sure you know what you are doing.

Globally, nearly two thirds of the world's population has access to a mobile phone[3]. This access is expected to grow even more over the next few years. The opportunities that this channel will provide global entrepreneurs will be incredible.

# Example: Online & Mobile Marketplaces

Don't let the fact that you don't have a website, a mobile app, or the money to launch one of them stop you from starting a business. Online marketplaces abound, ranging from auction behemoth eBay to specialists in handmade products like Etsy. Not only do they provide instant exposure; for a fee, they also provide the e-commerce transaction infrastructure for you. This is a great way to test your products to see if there is a large enough market for you to open your own online store. Companies like eBay, Amazon.com, Craigslist, and other sites have totally revolutionized the concept of commerce and made it easier for aspiring entrepreneurs to access the global marketplace.

Part of the success for many successful entrepreneurs and disruptors involves keeping it simple. For entrepreneurs who want to sell old or new products on eBay for example, simply register, submit a picture and a brief description, wait for bids, ship their products, and receive their payments, and they do all of this from the comfort of their homes. What could be easier? Platforms like this provide important tools for beginning entrepreneurs.

First, you can test just a single product online. Second, you have little or no advertising cost since the buyers are already looking on the site. Third, instead of trying to find a few buyers, you put your product into the global marketplace with all of its customers. Finally, these customers will bid on your product, so you don't have to fix your price, which provides you with immediate consumer feedback. You can quickly learn, adapt, and re-enter the market again with an enhanced version of your next product. A marketplace is comprised of both buyers and sellers, so be prepared for stiff competition. Provide the best-quality product, have realistic expectations, and then give it a try. For even more ideas check out sites like Etsy, which focuses on handmade products or Pinterest which is loaded with ideas from its user base.

Besides web-based businesses, don't forget about the mobile marketplace. I don't mean mobile apps; I mean businesses that literally move, such as the local ice cream truck, the home service providers, the sandwich trucks that show up at the construction sites, the dog groomers, vets or car detailers who make house calls, or the medical vans that visit rural communities. New entrants into this space include food trucks—specialty restaurants that enter new markets by supplying their products via trucks temporarily parked in key metro locations rather than buying or building physical locations. Being able to test or offer your products in multiple markets without investing in a "bricks and mortar" location has distinct advantages.

## Entrepreneurs & Disruptors: Go Global from Home

The following popular international websites have very quickly facilitated a dynamic global network and infrastructure for entrepreneurs and global business people. Since they are based outside the US, it is important for users to understand the terms and conditions of each of the sites and how they might affect your business.

### Global Websites

1. Baidu
2. QQ.com
3. Google India
4. Taobao
5. Yahoo! Japan[4]

## Mix & Match:

Besides selling products, one can also promote services via mobile or online channels. Frequently, developing a service is easier for an individual business startup compared with producing and selling a product. If it's your service, **you are the product**. You are in control of what skill you will provide, how it will be supplied, the price of the service (based on market feedback), and when and where the service will be delivered, unlike the creation or manufacturing of a product—which requires raw materials, storage, inventory management, production lead time, marketing, and more funding—if your product doesn't sell quickly. A service, on the other hand, can generally be started relatively fast with limited investment. The investment consists primarily of your time and some promotional effort.

What service can you provide?

To whom can you provide it?

At what price can you sell it?

How can you promote it?

## Your Ideas:

# Issue 19:   Co-ops, Barter, P2P, & Crowd Sourcing

Sector:      Culture & Society
Location:    US

## Issue: Eliminating the Middleman

As I mentioned earlier, providing products or services that are faster, cheaper, easier to use or provide fewer bells and whistles is a great way to penetrate market niches. Another way is to **simplify the process**. Eliminate the middleman by reducing the number of intermediaries or steps between the producer and the end-user. The greater the number of steps involved in the value chain, the greater the likelihood that the price will be higher, the process will be longer, the supply chain will be more complicated, and there will be more "handoffs" involved (increasing the chance for errors), resulting in less profit per step, especially for the original producer. Astute entrepreneurs and innovators have responded to this opportunity in many ways, and they continue to do so. Let's look at four models to see if they can inspire an idea.

### Cooperatives

According to the National Cooperative Business Association (NCBA), a co-op is defined as a "business controlled by their members—the people who use the co-op's services or buy its goods—not by outside investors...and return surplus revenues to members proportionate to their use of the cooperative..."[1].

Co-ops have been around for a long time. Most people are familiar with agricultural or rural utility co-ops, credit unions, or food and educational co-ops in urban neighborhoods. Co-ops can be large or small, and they can be found in almost any business sector, including energy, agriculture, financial services, education, healthcare, and worker-owned businesses. The NCBA states that there are nearly thirty thousand US cooperatives with $3 trillion in assets, and over 2 million jobs[2].

How can a co-op fit into your business idea? Besides streamlining the relationship between supplier and end-user, co-ops, along with their business alliances and networks, offer you strength in numbers or economies of scale without losing control. You can leverage this collective power to obtain benefits like increased purchasing power, shared technology, office space, support services, specialized expertise, and even employees. Co-ops can also provide access to distribution and business networks, banking services, and those all-important healthcare benefits. Sometimes it is better to develop your ideas with a group of like-minded colleagues rather than trying to do everything on your own.

**2012: International Year of Cooperatives**

The UN designated 2012 as the International Year of Cooperatives[3]. It is estimated that a billion people worldwide belong to cooperatives[4]. Co-ops can be especially effective in markets where a formal, entrepreneurial infrastructure is limited or non-existent.

# Opportunity: Barter

Another tool available to entrepreneurs and startups is bartering. *Barter* is another word for trade or exchange. You did it as a kid: "I will trade you two of my baseball cards for four of your football cards or three of my CDs for one of your DVDs."

Today, bartering has become more sophisticated and widespread. For small businesses or startups, bartering can help cash flow, reduce inventory, introduce your product to new customers, and help you obtain needed services. Since barter is typically a form of exchange without a formal currency be sure to check with a tax expert to ensure that you are in compliance with all regulations regarding bartering.

Using co-ops and barter can also be important options for individuals who have fallen on hard economic times, especially the unemployed or those who are trapped below the poverty line. Volunteer your time at a co-op in exchange for their products or services, or trade your skills with a willing service provider. Find a doctor, dentist, auto mechanic, tutor, or landlord and offer to design a website or landscaping plan, fix or build something, answer phones, organize the office, or build an app. Be creative and proactive—it may lead to a paying job or a new business idea.

## Example: Peer-to-Peer (P2P) Lending

Another way to eliminate intermediaries and link end-user needs directly to providers is through a P2P system. P2P was originally a concept describing a computer network matrix. Over the last few years, the P2P concept has expanded into the realm of human interaction. P2P systems can develop when a group or virtual community identifies a need and then organizes to provide a solution. One critical and frequent need for small businesses, entrepreneurs, and startups is access to seed, early-stage, or growth funding.

As a result of the last recession and the sluggish recovery, banks have been reluctant to loan money, especially to new or small businesses, regardless of their business performance. I have had a number of conversations with business owners with successful models who want to grow and hire more people but who have difficulties getting a loan. This is where P2P lending sites come into play.

These sites, which began appearing several years ago, may charge a fee to connect borrowers directly to a network of lenders who provide micro-loans as low as twenty-five dollars and depending on the model, the loans may or may not be repaid with established interest rates. This concept was reinforced by the passage of the Jobs Act in 2012, which allows for average citizens to invest directly in qualified smaller companies[5]. A great example of connecting peer lenders with startups is Kickstarter.com, which focuses on funding creative entrepreneurs. According to their site, over the last few years they have facilitated the funding of twenty-eight thousand projects[6].

## Entrepreneurs & Disruptors: Crowdsourcing

In my opinion, depending on the context, peer-to-peer and crowdsourcing can be very similar or virtually synonymous concepts, especially with regards to lending. However, beyond lending, crowdsourcing can be considered a slightly broader variation on this theme of directly connecting end-users or customer needs with service providers and problem-solvers. As the term indicates, using a crowd or community to provide you or your company with ideas, feedback, problem-solving, etc. can be a very effective, low-cost, and fast strategy for entrepreneurs. Another benefit is the opportunity to quickly build a like-minded and interested network of potential colleagues, customers, and community members.

## Mix & Match:

List the ideas or business models that you have and then select which ones could be developed using a co-op, bartering, P2P, or crowdsourcing model. Explain how it would work.

## Your Ideas:

# Issue 20: Cities & Towns—Reinvent Yourselves

Sector:     Demographics & Markets
Location:   US

## Issue: Small-Town America—A New Entrepreneurial Powerhouse

In addition to individuals, many cities and small towns throughout America have also become victims of the structural economic shifts that have occurred over the last few decades. These communities are now confronted with various economic dilemmas and, in more severe cases, basic survival. Due to budget cuts, reduced tax revenue, record-setting unemployment, plant closings, outsourcing, and shuttered businesses on main street, local labor forces, including recent graduates, are migrating to larger cities. These smaller cities and towns are faced with a critical economic decision. They must either reinvent themselves to attract the jobs and reinvigorate their economy, or they must watch their town slowly disappear. Just like many individuals, these cities and town are taking control of their destiny.

This dilemma is also an opportunity. First, with today's technology and connectivity, neither the size nor the location of a community has to be a barrier for entrepreneurs. According to the Federal Communications Commission, currently much of the US population already has access to at least a low-speed, wired broadband option[1]. Obviously, high-speed, wireless Internet would be preferable; however, with more providers, certain locations will at least be able to offer people a chance to stay in their community and operate online if they wish. For others who have grown tired of living in a large city and want to relocate to improve their quality of life, smaller towns are becoming more desirable and workable.

## Opportunity: Reinvent or Rebrand—Fast!

The second area of opportunity is for communities to reinvent and/or rebrand themselves. Many communities, especially smaller cities and towns, were typically dependent on one or two key industries for jobs, frequently agriculture and manufacturing. Today, with fewer farmers, outsourced manufacturing, productivity enhancements, and industry or facility consolidation, these jobs are gone, and they will not likely be replaced. The loss of high-paying jobs, youth migration, a population aging in place, and the all-important erosion of the tax revenue are common trends that are negatively impacting the economic and cultural base of many communities. Time is running out for many of these locations, and they need to respond to these issues.

**Just like individuals, no two communities are the same; each community is unique and can compete in interesting and effective ways.**

If you live in one of these communities, take a hard and honest look at your situation. What are your community's and your region's core competitive advantages? Historically, what have been your biggest success cases? What underutilized advantages do you have? What skill sets do you have in your talent pool? What can be easily, quickly, and/ or cost-effectively developed? What advantage does your location provide? What products and services are unique to your community or region? Do you have a vocational or community college or university nearby? Can you promote tourism based on historical events or famous residents?

# Example: "Pillars of the Community"

Community and business leaders, economic development specialists, citizens, and entrepreneurs must come together to drive this reinvention process. They must first recognize the problem—which is not always as easy as it sounds—identify solutions, and quickly design and facilitate an innovative environment to reinvent, retrain, and restructure key elements of the local economy. Starting a business incubator is one possible solution (See Issue 9: The 1% Innovation & Entrepreneur Fund).

According to the National Business Incubation Association, "Business incubation is a business support process that accelerates the successful development of startup and fledgling companies by providing entrepreneurs with an array of targeted resources and services"[2].

For the last several years, I have developed an interest in incubators as a way to jump-start and support startups. I have visited several incubators that are principally not-for-profit. Their objectives can vary based on location, supporting organization, and infrastructure. Their goals include diversifying and providing jobs for local economic development, transferring and/or commercializing university or corporate intellectual property, trading business support for equity in tech startups, supporting niche businesses for social entrepreneurship, and competing globally.

Each incubator is as unique as the individuals, organizations, or entities that manage and participate in their programs. Generally, they offer companies basic business support, including developing business plans; mentoring; providing free or subsidized office space; providing support for technical, legal, and financial issues; marketing; funding; providing support for human resources; sharing information; and networking. All of these elements are designed to launch and support successful and sustainable business models.

This model can be particularly effective if a manufacturing plant or business moves away from your city but leaves key employees behind.

These employees have valuable and unique training and skills, which, if linked to an incubator, the Small Business Administration, or another business support/resource center, could become a catalyst for launching several micro or small businesses back into the community.

A great source of information for cities and their citizens to reference as a checklist for developing a dynamic entrepreneurial environment can be found in a recent book by Brad Feld, entitled *Startup Communities – Building an Entrepreneurial Ecosystem in Your City.* A veteran investor and entrepreneur, he highlights the important elements which communities can use to develop and sustain a dynamic entrepreneurial economy[3].

# Entrepreneurs & Disruptors: Think Local

Whether out of necessity or by choice, it is becoming obvious that there is a growing movement among certain segments of Americans to support their community businesses and to think, grow, buy, and eat locally (see Issue 17: Local Food). The explosion of mobile devices has raised awareness surrounding the concept of community. People can now stay in constant touch, report their location, get real-time local offers, and stay informed about relevant local events. This is especially relevant to urban centers.

### Urban Renaissance

Like the people who are moving out of big cities, there are also people moving into city centers. These groups represent an interesting demographic mix ranging from young professionals, families, and creative types to empty-nesters who don't want the responsibilities of a large home and who enjoy the convenience of walking to restaurants, universities, cultural and sporting attractions. Workers who are tired of commuting also find living near the city center appealing. Obviously, focusing on this eclectic mix of people moving into and out of cities can be fertile ground for entrepreneurs.

## Mix & Match:

Identify the key challenges for your community. Now, describe the unique characteristics of your community and how you can use them as the basis to reinvent or rebrand your community.

## Your Ideas:

# Issue 21: Customer Relationships—The Core of Your Business?

Sector:     Demographics & Markets
Location:   US

## Issue: It's All About the Customer

Ideas and successful business models can originate with you or from
your customers. I have spent the majority of my business career
working in marketing, sales, and general management for well-known
global brands. The most important lesson I learned was the importance
of **customer relationships.** The likelihood for success is increased by
the ability of entrepreneurs and innovators to identify specific customer
segments and their unmet needs, to understand their behavior, and
to develop a business that develops their relationship. So, how do you
begin the process?

### LISTEN TO THE CUSTOMER!

It's common sense, right? What business would not listen to its
customers? Well, think of all of the businesses you interact with on
a daily basis. How many of them seem to be interested in what you
think? How many of them provide you with outstanding customer
service and thank you for your business? How many of them have
earned your loyalty?

# Opportunity: Customer Relationship Management (CRM)

My view is that CRM is business speak for developing a comprehensive business strategy for knowing who your customers are, listening to what they say, and developing the appropriate responses. Recently, the term has become synonymous with business-to-business (B2B) sales management tools and software; however, I will focus on a more comprehensive business-to-consumer (B2C) concept.

Successful businesses have practiced variations of CRM for generations. However, as many of them grew into larger companies, they seem to have forgotten the foundation for their success: the customer. Today, listening to your customers is more important than ever. Businesses are faced with the convergence of rapidly evolving global competition and real-time communication, which can lead to constant change and reinvention. In a 24/7 world, information, pricing, discounts, offers and images are distributed everywhere instantaneously, and the rules of the game change abruptly and continuously. If you have a good idea or business model, the chances are that several groups will quickly try to replicate your idea and compete with you. To survive, adapt, and stay ahead, you need immediate and constant feedback from your customers.

This is especially relevant given the new normal we seem to be experiencing after the recent recession. In response to the decline in customer spending during and after the downturn, many entrepreneurs, merchants, and business owners first cut costs and then turned to daily coupon companies to offer deep discounts to drive traffic. In my discussions with clients and friends, some of these discounts and strategies resulted in generating unprofitable results, which is not a sustainable model. This brings us back to CRM. If you follow some simple basic principles, your innovative ideas and business success can be driven by **what the customer really wants—not by what you think the customer needs**.

Based on my business experience, the vast majority of companies today continue to be **product-focused**. They develop products and services based on their view of customer demand. They are in constant pursuit of new customers to purchase the same products or marginally improved products from them. Faced with limited customer demand and growth, and increasing competitive and pricing pressure on their commodity products, companies in search of those precious new customers are finding customer acquisition increasingly more difficult and expensive. Some businesses innovate and launch new products but still remain trapped in their comfort zone with variations on the same theme. Those with no breakthrough products or customer loyalty begin a slow downward spiral, and may get purchased at a discount, file for bankruptcy, or simply disappear. Don't be one of them! This scenario is what can frequently happen during a normal business cycle. Now, look back at the challenges and outcomes faced by businesses between mid-2007 and today. What businesses do you know of that disappeared and why?

A **customer-focused** business, on the other hand, produces relevant products and services based on constant customer feedback and behavior. By seeking customer input, understanding it, and responding quickly, your business will be guided by customers and not by products. In this post-recession era with rapidly changing customer needs, behavior, spending patterns, and 24/7 competition, let your customers help you.

## Example: Recency—Frequency—Monetary (RFM)

Don't let the RFM concept scare you. It's really a common-sense model you can use to help you customize your own CRM strategy. It is something direct marketers have used for a long time. Basically, it asks some important questions. For example, when was the last time your best customers visited your store or website? How often do your best customers shop with you? How much do they typically spend in your business? How much will they spend throughout a lifetime of doing business with you?

Why are these questions important? They are important because they help you begin to understand and segment your customers and identify what you can do to deepen and maximize your relationship with them. Regardless of the size of your business or the technology or information you have available, you can use any or all of the following steps to manage your customer relationships and increase profitability. In full disclosure and as a shameless plug for my company, 4catalysts consulting, these are taken from my website at 4catalysts.com. I encourage my clients to utilize some or all of the following elements before spending a significant amount of time and money acquiring new customers. Develop your existing customer base first.

The steps are customer...

1. **Identification:** Collect whatever customer information you have available. Who are they? What do they buy? How often? How do they buy from you, online, mobile app, in store, by phone? Make sure to be transparent and let customers know what information you are collecting and what you are doing with that information. Customers need to trust your business if you want them to develop loyalty and a long-term relationship.

2. **Segmentation:** Compare your customer information with your product profitability segments to find your most profitable customers. Do the top 20 percent represent a significant portion of your profits? What about the bottom 20 percent?

3. **Retention:** Once you know your best customers, you can develop promotions to keep them coming back. You don't want to lose these valuable customers.

4. **Increase Revenue:** Motivate your best customers to increase their spending with you. Provide incentives for them to increase the amount of their transactions (up-sell) or purchase new items from you (cross-sell).

5. **Loyalty:** It is important to develop deep and long-lasting relationships with your best customers, since they will be valuable to your business for years to come (lifetime value). A loyalty program, if properly designed and operated, is an excellent tool.

6. **Reactivation:** Now that you have strategies for your best customers, you can begin to reactivate those who have left your business. Find out who the most profitable customers were and why they left—then get them back.

7. **Acquisition:** In a slow economy, many businesses spend more time and money trying to acquire new customers, which are usually less profitable in the short-term. Therefore, this strategy should generally be considered after you have maximized your efforts with your existing customer base.

## Entrepreneurs & Disruptors: Keep It Simple

I believe that the RFM and CRM strategies are two of the most powerful and cost-effective marketing and sales tools for any local or international business of almost any size. Ironically, they seem to be easy to understand yet one of the hardest strategies to execute. You don't have to spend millions of dollars on customer research, analytics, software, database infrastructure, and multi-channel advertising budgets. If you are an entrepreneur, a disruptor, a startup, or a small or medium-size business, keep it simple.

Here are some suggestions:

**Listen to your customers**—Talk to them, set up a suggestion box in your store, on your website, or call center. Conduct a weekly or monthly contest for the best idea, and reward customers and implement their ideas quickly. Select individual or small groups of customers and set aside time for a brief feedback session to measure your pricing, product quality, and customer service, and to seek new business ideas.

**Get them to come back more often**—Start simple. First, focus on delivering good value, and consistent, quality customer service. Try to give customers a physical, online, or mobile punch card or discount coupon to return frequently or bounce back to your business. Do your math. Find out what makes sense for your business. This is an investment in long-term customer frequency—and hopefully customer loyalty—and it could pay you big dividends over time.

**Ask their permission**—Over time, a customer who trusts you will give you permission to communicate and develop a relationship with them. Eventually, they will allow you to offer them customized promotions or incentives via their preferred channel. Again, start simple. Send your customers an incentive during the week or month of their birthday or anniversary.

**Recognize your best customers**—In my experience, a minority of your customers will likely represent a majority of your revenue and profit. Not only do you need to know who they are and listen to them; you must also recognize what they do for your business and frequently thank them for this. In this post-recession new normal, you can no longer afford to spend the money and do the hard work of acquiring new customers and then take them for granted. Again, do your math. Give them special offers, open up your store or website for special VIP events, or provide them with unique experiences. Be creative—these are your best customers and they should be treated as such.

## Mix & Match:

Divide your customer base into your own segments and keep it simple. Use the definition that makes the most sense for your business (e.g., age, gender, location, money spent, web, mobile, store). Now, what do you think are the unique needs of each segment? Is your business meeting them? Now, confirm your assumptions directly with your customers.

## Your Ideas:

# Issue 22: Big Challenges—Big Ideas— Big Opportunities

Sector:     Culture & Society
Location:   US


## Issue: Have a Big Idea? We Could Use One...or Two!

Most of the issues covered so far have been focused on the opportunity for entrepreneurs and innovators to select a customer need or an underserved market and then consider starting a full-time or part-time business. However, these days the US also faces huge challenges that require some game changing ideas. The irony of these persistent challenges is that we have the knowledge, the personnel, the expertise, the technology, and, yes, even the money to resolve many of these issues. What is missing is the environment, the commitment, and the leadership to inspire innovative public/private sector brainstorming and collaboration, and the creation of new operating models to resolve these issues, create millions of new jobs, and regain a leadership role both in key sectors of the economy and in global competitiveness. We need to build more effective, functional links and collaboration between Main street, Wall street and Government street.

Take three key components of our economy that impact all of us: infrastructure, education, and healthcare. These are massive sectors that are essential to our future success and employment. Although the sectors all still function, their performance and effectiveness have been degrading over time, and, when benchmarked against other global competitors, they have significantly fallen behind. We need some new, innovative and game changing business models that can be quickly jump-started and that can leverage the cutting-edge technological advancements that are available today. The speed of change is accelerating and we as individuals, entrepreneurs, corporate businesses, and even politicians have to adapt quickly and to collaborate and launch breakthrough solutions.

## Opportunity: Infrastructure

According to The American Society of Civil Engineers' *2013 Report Card for America's Infrastructure,* the US received an overall grade of D+. They estimate that a five-year, $3.6 trillion investment will be needed to upgrade our infrastructure. Those categories that received some type of D grade include:

| | |
|---|---|
| Aviation | Dams |
| Drinking & Wastewater | Energy |
| Hazardous Waste | Inland Waterways |
| Levees | Roads |
| Schools | Transit[1] |

So, who can come up with new business models that address D-level infrastructure (high demand), declining federal, state, and local budgets (limited public funding), high unemployment in the construction industry (dormant, readily available skilled labor, equipment, and materials), corporate cash surplus (available private funding), and technological advancement (new processes and materials)? Local bond elections may not always work like they have in the past. To innovate and to get things moving more quickly, we need to look into alternative funding strategies—crowd-funded, private equity, individual, corporate consortia, joint ventures, build for equity, toll or pay-for-usage, revenue-sharing, tax incentives, and advertising or sponsorship scenarios-for example.

# Example: Education

As I indicated in Issue 10 on graduation rates, globally the US has fallen to 14th in reading, 17th in math, and 25th in science[2]. In 2013, this can no longer be acceptable. We are leaving millions of children behind, creating vast new groups of long-term unemployed and depriving our society and our economy of the potential contributions of this valuable and talented student segment, exactly at the time when we need more innovators, designers and builders of things. In good economic times, dropouts and those with questionable skills have had difficulty getting jobs, but during a prolonged jobless recovery, this challenge becomes significantly more difficult.

Today's schools are faced with multiple problems. Does your community face any of the following challenges?

- A chronic shortage of qualified and motivated teachers
- Overcrowded classrooms
- Unequal spending per student
- More children slipping through the cracks
- Increased crime
- More students graduating without the basic skills
- Exploding college costs

So, what can you do? As a parent, you can get involved in your local school as a teacher, administrator, board member, PTA member, volunteer aide, tutor, or counselor. As an entrepreneur you can work to provide alternative educational models like skill-based versus age-based or grade-based approaches, flexible graduation plans for gifted and/or students with learning differences, or special programs within school curricula that permit students to concentrate on specific career paths like the travel and leisure industry, technology, medicine, vocational programs, science, engineering or entrepreneurship.

As discussed in the infrastructure section, entrepreneurs can develop new and innovative educational models, or they can improve on the best practices that have already been launched around the country.

Entrepreneurs can have a positive impact by focusing on effective teachers who are experienced, motivated, and well compensated (imagine if teachers could supplement their incomes with discounts at key businesses), smaller class sizes, greater individualized instruction, innovative online learning modules, earlier detection of learning or attendance issues, more equitable and efficient educational spending, and greater security in schools.

Entrepreneurs, disruptors and innovators who can take existing models and change or improve them to become more effective, efficient, faster, easier, and less expensive—or change them to meet market needs—may do well and make a positive difference in the lives of children, their families, and their communities. Are there opportunities in some of the following alternative school models?

Charter Schools
Home Schooling
Online Learning
- 24/7 access to curricula, teachers, and tutors
- No geographical, age or time of day limitations
- Lower cost for students and lower contact cost per student
- Individualized instruction to focus on user's needs & skills
- Unique curricula or approaches to learning

## Entrepreneurs & Disruptors: Healthcare

As I highlighted in Issue 15 on Healthcare, there is probably no industry that is more ready for disruptive innovation than the healthcare industry. We have the costliest healthcare system in the world, but compared with other developed nations, the US underperforms on several key categories[3].

Healthcare is an extraordinarily complex business model that has many constituents, but innovators who discover and launch new or improve on existing delivery, access, preventative, technology or payment models that meet rapidly growing demand or improve performance or enhance productivity may be handsomely rewarded.


## Mix & Match:


In addition to infrastructure, education, and healthcare, what other national or regional challenges, vulnerable business or operating models need big ideas to fix them?



What additional competitive differentiators or disruptors can you identify? Products or services that:

Are less expensive

Contain unique inputs

Are simpler to understand or use

Benefit from more efficient production processes

Have supply-chain/logistical advantages

Provide better customer service

Have less quality or functionality for less money

Benefit from unique funding or ownership models

**Your Ideas:**

# Part Four

## WHAT: GLOBAL ISSUES & TRENDS

Many of the economic and business trends in the new normal are not limited to just the US. Part Four focuses on **globalization** and the importance for global citizens, companies, and entrepreneurs to understand international trends and potential opportunities. Globalization is much more than the outsourcing of jobs or free trade. Today, there are very few things in our lives that are not dependent on global events or issues. Understanding international events, cultures, and their relationship to you, your family, your job—or lack thereof—and your community is no longer a luxury; it is becoming a necessity. Given today's technology, information, and communication channels, becoming a entrepreneur or an innovator and solving a problem or starting a new business in your home country is not as difficult as you might imagine. The following are a few trends to consider in a world of opportunities.

# Issue 23:   Global Unemployment

Sector:       Business & Finance
Location:     Global

## Issue: It's Not Just an American Problem!

The impact of the last US recession was quickly felt around the world. The effects of the worst economic downturn since the Great Depression varied across regions, with many developed and European economies being the hardest hit. In early 2013, parts of Europe continued to be mired in a recession. Just as in the US, one indicator of the health of the global economy is the relationship between the economic recovery and global unemployment.

According to the International Monetary Fund, prior to the recession, world output was growing around 4 percent annually, and then it actually declined 0.5 percent in 2009, which may have been the first time that happened since World War II[1]. Although most international economies encountered less severity and a quicker recovery than the US did, many economies continued to be plagued by the same dilemma: a jobless recovery. The economic forecast for 2013 is subject to both great speculation and a host of macro and micro-economic factors.

What has been the economic impact of this on unemployment? According to the International Labour Organization (ILO), at around 6 percent, the global unemployment rate in 2012 remained stubbornly high compared to 5.5 percent unemployment in 2007. It is estimated that the world needs to create 200 million jobs to recover from the recession[2].

## Opportunity: Global Unemployment Rates

Let's take a look at the regions tracked by the ILO's, "Global Employment Trends 2012," for an estimate of the 2011 global unemployment rates.

| ILO Regions | % Unemployment Rate |
| --- | --- |
| World | 6.0% |
| Developed Economies & The European Union | 8.5 |
| Non-EU Europe & CIS | 8.6 |
| E. Asia | 4.1 |
| SE Asia & Pacific | 4.7 |
| S. Asia | 3.8 |
| Latin Am. & Caribbean | 7.2 |
| Middle East | 10.2 |
| N. Africa | 10.9 |
| Sub-Saharan Africa | 8.2[2] |
| | |
| United States (2012, December) | 7.8%[3] |

Other than the low unemployment rates in parts of Asia, the rest of the world is hampered by rates that are between 7 and 11%. Depending on the accuracy of the data and the formula for calculating unemployment—as we can see in the US—in some cases, these rates may be understated.

# Example: Youth Unemployment (UE)

High youth unemployment is a problem on many levels. For recent graduates, it is frustrating to have few or no job opportunities and potentially reduced lifetime earnings even though they have received training. For a country unable to benefit from its most recently educated labor pool, it is a tragically untapped resource, while a growing youth unemployment problem can potentially lead to increased crime, civil unrest or political confrontation.

Again, using the ILO's numbers for 2011, except for parts of Asia, youth unemployment ranges from 13 to 27%. What is worse is that, like in the US, many disillusioned individuals may no longer be actively seeking work, and they have therefore dropped out of the labor pool and are no longer counted in the unemployment rate. Therefore, it is likely that some of these numbers are understated.

| ILO Regions | Youth UE (%)* |
|---|---|
| World | 12.7% |
| Developed Economies & The European Union | 17.9 |
| Non-EU Europe & CIS | 17.7 |
| East Asia | 8.8 |
| Southeast Asia & the Pacific | 13.4 |
| South Asia | 9.9 |
| Latin America & the Caribbean | 13.3 |
| The Middle East | 26.2 |
| North Africa | 27.1 |
| Sub-Saharan Africa | 12.8[4] |
| **United States** (October 2012) | |
| 16–19 years | 23.5 |
| 20–24 | 12.7[5] |

*Projections: 2012

# Entrepreneurs & Disruptors: Startup Weekend

Growing and long-term unemployment are examples of the new normal, even on a global basis. Current economic growth in many countries is not generating sufficient jobs for many growing populations. For a variety of reasons, it is apparent that governments, corporations, and institutions are unable to provide all of the leadership and employment that is needed for the future. As with the US, this global paradigm shift will yield a new wave of involuntary entrepreneurs, innovators, and disruptors.

In economies with strong entrepreneurial infrastructure, startup educational programs, incubators, accelerators, boot camps, and co-working spaces can be powerful catalysts. I saw this power in action over a couple of days when I participated in a Startup Weekend event in Dallas, Texas. Within fifty-four hours, I saw several ideas presented, designed, developed, launched, and presented to a team of venture capitalists and angel investors. It was an awesome display of talent, teamwork, collaboration, and high-speed productivity. As a model, it is one solution that is being applied globally by the folks at Startup Weekend. In November 2012, they were sponsoring a Global Startup Battle in an estimated 140 locations worldwide. Check them out at: http://startupweekend.org/.

For economies without an entrepreneurial infrastructure, mentoring, apprenticeships and internships will also be important as well as peer-to-peer support, both domestically and globally (see Issue 19: Co-ops, Barter, P2P, & Crowdsourcing).

## Mix & Match:

For **local** entrepreneurs, list:

Specific barriers to job creation in your country and your community

Some unmet needs of the people in your country and your community

Elements missing in your community to create a dynamic entrepreneurial environment

Your industry, functional, product, and service expertise

Your special talents and interests

Products or services you could develop that can be sold online

For **international** entrepreneurs, list:

Countries of interest

Countries you have visited or countries where you have contacts

Skills you have that can help develop an entrepreneurial environment

Languages you speak

Your business network that could provide "peer-to-peer" support

Industry expertise

Functional expertise

Product or service expertise

Special talents or interests

## Your Ideas:

# Issue 24:   Top 10 Entrepreneurial Nations

Sector:         Business & Finance
Location:       Global


## Issue: Voluntary or Involuntary?

Entrepreneurship is a key catalyst in the global new normal. It sparks innovation, stimulates economic growth, creates jobs, develops traditional and disruptive competition, launches productivity enhancements, and improves competitiveness. As discussed previously, entrepreneurship can be **voluntary** or **involuntary**.

Voluntary entrepreneurs flourish when infrastructure, support, technology, and funding are made readily available to capable and motivated risk-takers regardless of their age, gender, culture, or level of education.

Involuntary entrepreneurs are driven by necessity. For individuals in transition, unemployed graduates, people who are long-term unemployed, and people in developing economies or disrupted industries where job options have been reduced or never created, entrepreneurship might be viewed as a less-preferred but necessary choice for job creation.

# Opportunity: The Top 10

Which countries are the most entrepreneurial in the world in 2012? According to the Global Entrepreneurship and Development Index (GEDI), they were:

## 10 Most Entrepreneurial Nations

1.    US
2.    Sweden
3.    Australia
4.    Iceland
5.    Denmark
6.    Canada
7.    Switzerland
8.    Belgium
9.    Norway
10.   Netherlands/Taiwan[1]

Based on my research and travel, emerging pockets of entrepreneurial activity exist almost everywhere. Here are a few more markets that I would keep my eye on.

## Entrepreneurial Hotspots

Chile
Poland
Czech Republic
South Africa
Israel
Turkey
Malaysia
Singapore

# Example: Market Selection—The Andes

To identify opportunities, look for unique characteristics in specific market segments and then narrow your focus. For example, let's assume that you are a bilingual English/Spanish-speaking importer or food entrepreneur looking to introduce new or distinctive food products.

First, you could narrow your global market search to Latin America and the Caribbean. Then you could focus on areas with unique crop (fruits, vegetables, coffee, wine, flowers etc.) environments, and growing seasons. Next, you could further narrow your selection to the areas surrounding the Andes mountain range with its myriad microclimates and unique products. Let's also assume that you have commercial contacts in Asia. Chile and Peru, with their ports, trade access, and Asian business network, would become priorities to consider.

# Entrepreneurs & Disruptors: The Value Chain & Process Improvement

Besides being different, simpler or cheaper, process improvement or process streamlining can also be competitively advantageous. Let's assume that you have found your unique Chilean or Peruvian agricultural product, and after analyzing the value chain (the processes and financial flows from grower to end user), you have identified several opportunities for improving productivity, increasing speed-to-market, and generating better financial returns for the producers. For example:

- A minor process improvement in transportation could improve one's speed-to-market, increase revenue for fresher products, and deliver higher profits because of reduced costs.

- By dealing directly with an exporter, reducing one broker from the process could significantly improve revenue for the grower.

- The addition of a key piece of equipment, such as a mountainside conveyor belt, an irrigation system, or a small refrigeration truck, could increase the yield and quality for a longer sales cycle.

- A small group of growers with the right tools or organizing as a cooperative (see Issue 19: Co-ops) could become more competitive, helping both their families and their community.

## Mix & Match:

Fill in the relevant categories below and then randomly mix them to generate ideas.

Countries you are interested in

Countries in which you have contacts

Languages you speak

Industry expertise you have

Functional expertise you have

Product expertise you have

Service expertise you have

## Your Ideas:

# Issue 25:   Water Management

Sector:     Environment
Location:   Global

## Issue: Water, Water Everywhere and Not a Drop to Waste

If the majority of the earth's surface is made up of water then what's the problem? Given the increasing demand for this critical natural resource, the lack of effective management and infrastructure, conservation and environmental protection are some of the problems which need solutions to ensure global access to a consistent, clean and safe water supply.

### Supply

According to the United Nations, the world's water supply is broken down as 97.5 percent salt water and only **2.5 percent fresh water,** of which:

- 70% is frozen in glaciers and polar icecaps (global warming may change this).
- 30% is soil moisture, in underground aquifers, or groundwater.

Only **0.3 percent of freshwater** can be found in lakes, rivers, and reservoirs, and not all of this water is easily accessible[1].

To complicate matters, this accessible freshwater is not evenly distributed. The great equalizer is the climate. Evaporation and precipitation make water available on a sustainable basis. With the warming of the planet and more frequent episodes of extreme weather (See Issue 12: Extreme Weather), managing the supply and demand of water is growing more challenging. Although water availability or scarcity may change based on weather patterns, there are parts of the world that are more frequently affected by water scarcity such as: central & southern Asia, North Africa, the southwestern US and northern Mexico, the Middle East and parts of Australia[2].

The biggest challenge for water management centers on cities where a significant portion of the world's population live. The issues of providing and managing safe drinking water and clean sanitation systems will be ongoing challenges for decades, and they represent potentially significant opportunities for entrepreneurs and innovators with effective solutions.

## Demand

Today, freshwater usage can be broken down into three broad categories. As you can see, the agricultural and industrial sectors represent 92 percent of water usage. Even a small improvement in efficiency or effectiveness in one of these sectors could have a significantly positive impact on water management and conservation.

### Basic Water Usage Sectors

- 70% irrigation
- 22% industry
- 8% domestic households[3]

As global populations increase and economic development improves around the world, the global demand for water will also increase. According to the UN, water usage is expected to increase by 50 percent and 18 percent, respectively, in developing and developed countries by 2025[3]

The domestic household usage of water is where most individuals have the best opportunity for developing their own personal water management programs. For example, a US household uses approximately sixty-nine gallons of water each day, which is broken down as follows:

| | |
|---|---|
| Toilets | 26.7 % |
| Clothing | 21.7 % |
| Showers | 16.8 % |
| Faucets | 15.7 % |
| Leaks | 13.7 % |
| Other | 5.3 %[4] |

A cost-effective, new product, service, or process to reduce water usage, anyone? Anyone?

## Opportunity: Wait—You Can't Drink That !

According to statistics from the Center for Disease Control and Prevention, the impact of unsafe drinking water is staggering.

- 780 million people don't have access to improved drinking water sources.
- Potentially 9 percent of global diseases and 6 percent of global deaths could be prevented by providing access to safe water and practicing safe sanitation and proper hygiene,
- 800,000 children, under the age of five die each year from diarrheal diseases[5]

Although progress continues to be made in filtration and well-digging technologies and applications, there is still much to be done to reduce the cost of these lifesaving techniques. Much also needs to be done to provide access to them, as well as deploying and maintaining them.

## Example: Desalination—The Other 97.5%

The logical place to look for a big solution to limited fresh water is at the world's oceans. Removing salt from seawater has typically been an expensive and complicated process, but given technological improvements, falling prices, and growing demand, the desalination industry is growing quickly.

Domestically, there are several hundred desalination plants in the US. As one might expect, many of these plants are located in coastal states like Florida, California and Texas. Internationally the Middle East continues to be the leader in the industry[6]. What about developing technology and desalination products that can be cost-effectively produced and made widely available at prices that a community or even a family could afford?

## Entrepreneurs & Disruptors: It's Raining Opportunities!

Opportunities abound to improve global water management including:

More accurate data
Improved agriculture practices
Conservation
Preventing saltwater intrusion
Pollution prevention
Infrastructure repair
Low flow equipment
Water rights
Collection of rain water
Drip irrigation
Wastewater treatment and recycling
Sustainable landscape design
Smart buildings
New pricing and metering

# Mix & Match

Select your areas of interest and expertise from above and decide where you might be able to apply them.

# Your Ideas

# Issue 26: Brazil—Emerging Middle Class & World-Class Events

Sector:      Demographics & Markets
Location:    Global

## Issue: Tudo Bem?

For most international investors, the acronym BRICs has become quite familiar. It stands for the global markets of Brazil, Russia, India, and China. Of the almost 7 billion inhabitants of our planet, these four countries represent an estimated 2.9 billion people, or 41 percent of the earth's population.

| Country | Population Rank | Population (millions) |
|---------|----------------|----------------------|
| China   | 1              | 1,343                |
| India   | 2              | 1,205                |
| Brazil  | 5              | 206                  |
| Russia  | 9              | 138[1]               |

For global entrepreneurs, it is important to understand the significance of these countries. First, each country by itself is a huge market. Second, they have all had explosive growth over the last several years, even during the US recession. Third, they have large emerging, middle-class, consumer segments. Fourth, they have drawn a lot of attention from multinational corporations, which have invested significant capital and assets into these markets to access future consumer spending. Finally, these countries have also invested substantial resources in their own markets to meet the needs of their emerging middle classes and to become more globally competitive.

Brazil is a great example of the types of opportunities that exist in many emerging markets. Today, it is estimated that slightly over half the population is now included in the middle class[2]. With economic progress, these consumers tend to increase their spending with both local and international businesses. Much of this spending can be found in the largest cities.

| Largest Cities | Population (millions) |
|---|---|
| Sao Paulo | 20.0 |
| Rio de Janeiro | 11.8 |
| Belo Horizonte | 5.7 |
| Porto Alegre | 4.0 |
| Brasilia (capital) | 3.8[3] |

The exploding middle class represents an opportunity for both local and global entrepreneurs. Because of the sheer size of Brazil's population, when a percentage of people move out of poverty and into the middle class, the market potential can be substantial. According to government studies, between 1999 and 2009, an estimated 31 million people entered the Brazilian middle class[4].

The challenges and opportunities in emerging markets are numerous, primarily due to the inability of local businesses to grow as quickly as demand does. Although these businesses eventually catch up, entrepreneurs and international businesses try to fill in the gap, especially in areas like global brands, local retail, education, commodities, energy, and the food and beverage sector.

# Opportunity: 2014 World Cup—Goooooooooal!

Brazil is preparing to host two of the great events in sports, the 2014 World Cup soccer tournament and the 2016 Summer Olympics. In addition to the recognition and revenue that will be generated, the investment and preparation for these marquis events will be considerable. The World Cup will be held in the summer in multiple cities around the country. As we have seen when countries host major events like this, there are generally significant investments in infrastructure projects like public transport, roads, stadiums, and airport projects.

Think about other opportunities for local and even multinational entrepreneurs. Some key sectors to consider are:

- Tourism—cultural, historical and ecological tours, lodging, and restaurants
- Transportation—taxis and shuttles
- Construction
- Engineering
- Souvenirs/clothing—event-related and country-related souvenirs and clothes that are sold in shops or online
- Retail
- Consulting
- Music and entertainment
- Handicrafts

# Example: Rio's 2016 Summer Olympics—Is Samba a Sport?

For the 2016 Olympics, Rio de Janeiro is targeting billions of dollars for an extreme makeover. Just like the World Cup, the goal is to improve and expand the infrastructure. It is estimated that over US $20 billion will be spent on projects that include hotel and restaurant construction and transport infrastructure[5]. Engineering and consulting firms will play a key role in providing opportunities to participate in the infrastructure projects.

## Entrepreneurs & Disruptors: Demographic Opportunities—and Oil

Brazil's growing economy also provides multiple opportunities for entrepreneurs. Here are some market segment opportunities, based on demographics.

- Due to a declining trend in population growth rates, Brazil's aging population is expected to grow substantially over the next several decades leading to opportunities similar to those in the US: health and home care and pension management[6] (see Issue 11: Baby Boomer Market).

- After living in South America and working in the financial services sector throughout Latin America and the Caribbean for many years, I was always impressed with the number of people, in some markets, who were unbanked or did not have some type of formal banking relationship. With Brazil's emerging middle class and an estimated 244 million mobile phone users[7] a huge opportunity for mobile financial transactions would appear to exist.

- Finally, another area to watch is Brazil's energy sector. Given the significant discoveries of offshore oil reserves and the complicated process involved in turning those reserves into production, this sector represents opportunities as well[8].

## Mix & Match:

Do you speak Portuguese or Spanish?

Have you traveled to Brazil or Latin America?

What do you know about Brazilian culture?

Do you have friends or family who live in Brazil?

Would you like to travel to Brazil?

Do you have expertise in any of the sectors highlighted in this chapter?

Tudo Bem!

## Your Ideas:

# Issue 27:   Global Competitiveness

Sector:        Business & Finance
Location:     Global

## Issue: Global Competition Is Heating Up— Don't Get Left Behind!

Global competitiveness is a major and somewhat complex component affecting both employment and entrepreneurship. If your region or country is extremely competitive, the chances are that your business, financial, legal, regulatory, educational, and operational infrastructure are well developed and functioning efficiently, which one assumes would lead to a robust job and entrepreneurial environment. However, it may also indicate a highly productive, efficient, and globally interconnected economy where many jobs may be automated, outsourced, and/or lost to industry consolidation.

If your region or country is less competitive, then entrepreneurial or informal business activities may be favored in response to unmet local needs, the lack of locally produced goods, services, and jobs, and/or the need to design and develop the legal, technological, and physical infrastructure necessary for greater global competitiveness. In either environment, entrepreneurs, innovators, and disruptors who can quickly identify opportunities and respond accordingly could do well.

Each year, the World Economic Forum, in conjunction with experts from around the world, produces the Global Competitiveness Report, which is an excellent and comprehensive analysis of this issue. Check out the latest report to see where countries you are interested in rank[1].

## Opportunity: The World Is Getting Smaller-Flatter-More Interdependent

The pace of globalization and interdependence is accelerating. Accessing and applying sophisticated communication, information, transportation and technology continue to make global integration, collaboration and competition more readily achievable.

Quantum leaps in progress are popping up everywhere. In emerging markets, farmers use GPS devices, children access the Internet, government protests get organized using mobile devices, villages bypass land lines for cell phone service, and solar panels bring energy to remote locations.

This combination of rapidly accelerating technological linkages and interdependence is leading to greater challenges and opportunities. Each individual, region, and country is uniquely impacted, and therefore they will react and compete differently. Before the new normal, a common phrase in business was to "think globally and act locally." Entrepreneurs and innovators may consider taking this statement a step further and to "think globally and act individually"— at the consumer level. It's all about you and your relationship with your domestic or international counterpart or customer (see Issue 21: Customer Relationships).

## Example: Research & Development

There are several metrics available to gauge the progress of countries with respect to global competitiveness and innovation. Some good indicators include the number of patents issued, the amount of money spent on R&D, and the number of specialized graduates each year. Although in the US, industry funds an estimated two-thirds of R&D, it is important for aspiring entrepreneurs and others to understand that the federal government through universities, foundations and local government is also a great source of R&D funding[2].

# Entrepreneurs & Disruptors: Ease of Doing Business

Entrepreneurs, regardless of the competitive infrastructure, must understand how easy or how difficult it is to start a business in a given country. In yet another list, the World Bank's "Doing Business 2011" measures how much time and capital are needed to start a business, as well as the number of processes that are required, and then it ranks the countries based on these factors. Most of the countries at the top of the list typically have stable governments and strong, functioning business infrastructure[3].

Given more entrepreneurial-friendly infrastructure, regulations, and reduced barriers to starting or running a business in these countries, an established or more risk-averse entrepreneur may be more attracted to countries at the top of these rankings. For the disruptors, risk-takers, or those who are very familiar with the environment of emerging markets or developing economies in the middle or at the bottom of the list, the challenges, as well as the opportunities, may be larger. For entrepreneurs and disruptors who can find the right balance between the right markets, the hot sectors and the barriers to entry, a world of opportunities exist.

## Mix & Match:

Answer the following questions from your point of view:

How much risk can I tolerate?

How much experience do I have with starting or running a business?

What are my countries of interest?

How do these countries rank on competitiveness?

How do these countries rank on the ease of doing business?

How do these countries rank on entrepreneurialism?

How well do I understand each of the markets that I am interested in?

Do I understand the legal and regulatory issues?

What languages do I speak?

What industry/functional expertise do I have?

What product/service expertise do I have?

What are my unique talents or skills?

## Your Ideas:

# Issue 28: Markets at the Bottom of the Pyramid

Sector:     Demographics & Markets
Location:   Global

## Issue: The Bottom of the Pyramid

> These unhappy times call for the building of plans that rest upon the forgotten, the unorganized but the indispensable units of economic power, for plans like those of 1917, that build from the bottom up and not from the top down, that put their faith once more in the forgotten man at the bottom of the economic pyramid.
>
> —President Franklin D. Roosevelt

One of the biggest challenges for both large and small businesses is maintaining profitable growth. Since most businesses are product-focused (see Issue 21: Customer Relationships), they must constantly find new markets and customers for their products or services. For large companies, this means entering global markets, and for multinational companies, who are already there, it means entering new market segments, such as those with less income, sometimes referred to as the bottom or base of the pyramid (BOP). Having spent part of my career in international business opening up markets in both developed and developing countries, I can attest to both the opportunities and challenges involved in such a strategy.

165

## Opportunity: 4 Billion People

According to the World Resource Institute, which published an excellent resource entitled the *Next 4 Billion*, those individuals at the BOP who live on only a few dollars a day represent a dynamic and growing, multi-trillion dollar, underserved market[1].

Nobody has done more to call attention to this market segment than C.K. Prahalad in his compelling work *The Fortune at the Bottom of the Pyramid—Eradicating Poverty Through Profits*. In his book, he not only defines the size and scope of these unique market opportunities, but he also goes into great detail about how to most effectively address the unmet needs of the various segments included in this global market[2].

## Example: Each Market Is Unique

As a business executive who has traveled around the world, I realized early on that each market must be understood at the local level. One of the first mistakes that businesses make is to treat international markets as extensions of their home market, which leads to another mistake: thinking that businesses can break into these markets simply by introducing or tweaking products or services that were successful in their home markets.

Before I address these mistakes, let's look at the size and scope of these BOP markets to better understand them. The size of the opportunities in the various industries in the BOP market varies, but they are significant and very interesting. These are multi-billion dollar sectors ranging from food and energy to housing and healthcare to name a few.

Another fast-growing sector is the area of financial services for the unbanked. When you combine the innovative financial strategies being developed with the explosion of mobile device usage around the world, you can see another example of the opportunities for quantum leaps in innovation and disruption.

# Entrepreneurs & Disruptors: Success Factors

Now, let's try and identify some mistakes made by businesses hoping to break into the BOP markets. Based on my corporate experience trying to enter new or expand existing international markets, I learned several lessons. The unique characteristics and needs of the local consumer demand specific and relevant product features. If you are a foreign entrepreneur or company trying to enter an international market, make sure you adapt your model to meet local needs and customs, especially in the areas of: pricing, product size or functionality, real estate requirements and locations, sales and marketing campaigns and branding, purchasing options, distribution and logistics and, of course, management. These may all seem like common sense, but you would be surprised at how many businesses, both large and small, have failed to sufficiently adapt to the local market.

## Mix & Match:

Match countries or market segments with the following industry sectors to see where you could apply one of the success factors.

Sectors
Food
Energy
Housing
Transportation
Health
IT
Water
Financial services

## Your Ideas:

# Issue 29:   Social Entrepreneurs

Sector:       Culture & Society
Location:     Global


## Issue: UN Millennium Development Goals

In 1987, I received my PhD in international studies. One of my areas
of study was economic development. At that time, I assumed that
within twenty-five years the world would have resolved many of its
critical social problems. Although the world has made substantial
progress, there is still much to do. In many cases, traditional thinking
and top-down solutions are not always the most effective solutions.
Enter the social entrepreneur with innovative and disruptive, bottom-
up approaches.

One way to identify the most pressing global social issues is to look at
the list prepared by the UN. In 2002, the UN started the Millennium
Project to combat key issues regarding poverty, hunger, and disease that
affects billions of people. They set a 2015 deadline to accomplish their
targets.

The Millennium Development Goals are to:

- Eradicate extreme hunger and poverty
- Achieve universal primary education
- Promote gender equality and empower women
- Reduce child mortality
- Improve maternal health

- Combat HIV/AIDS, malaria, and other diseases
- Ensure environmental sustainability
- Develop a global partnership for development[1]

As you might imagine, progress on these issues is mixed. Although there are exceptions in every region, generally there are still a multitude of opportunities for entrepreneurs, innovators and disruptors and their ideas and business models to make a positive difference in the world.

## Opportunity: Medical Hotspots

Another source for identifying troubled parts of the world that are in need of innovative problem-solving—in this case, emergency medical care—is the work that is being done by the myriad of non-governmental organizations (NGOs) and foundations around the world. On their website and in their alerts and fundraising material, these organizations list the areas where they are running operations.

Anyone on the front lines battling a natural disaster or a humanitarian or medical emergency is always on the lookout for creative and innovative solutions that can be easily and cost-effectively deployed on a large scale to provide better and broader security and care for those impacted.

## Example: Success Factors

Based on my travels, research and work in developing economies, I believe keys to success should include a comprehensive toolkit and support in order to jumpstart and sustain economic development. This is very similar to what is needed for aspiring entrepreneurs worldwide (see Issue # 9: on Incubators, Accelerators …)Today, it appears that the most successful solutions are those that are developed in conjunction with and implemented and maintained by the local community.

## Entrepreneurs & Disruptors: More Success Factors

Another great source for identifying areas of need and country-specific indicators of progress is the World Bank, which tracks eighteen key topics, including agriculture, education, energy, poverty, etc.[2]. As I mentioned earlier, it is not necessary that an entrepreneur, innovator or disruptor has to have a unique idea or be the first to apply a model, process or concept to be successful. On the contrary, the world is full of brilliant, innovative, fully-functioning success stories already deployed. They are just waiting to be customized if needed, or scaled to increase results and/or access. Start with them.

## Mix & Match:

Which of these successful qualities do you possess? Now, compare these qualities to the social issues that you care strongly enough about to make a positive change.

## Your Ideas:

# Issue 30:   India & China: Emerging Giants

Sector:        Science & Technology
Location:      Global

## Issue: The Tide Is Turning

This book would not be complete without a few words about the
"I" and the "C" in BRIC. For years, many Americans have known
India and China to be places that benefit from the outsourcing of
jobs. However, these countries have also quickly developed large,
sophisticated companies and experienced rapid urbanization, increased
consumer spending, huge emerging middle classes, and explosive
economic growth. This is especially important to the global economy
and has implications for the US economy as well, given that these two
countries represent more than a third of the world's population (see
Issue 26: Brazil—Emerging Middle Class & World-Class Events).

## Opportunity: Booming Economic Growth

To counter-balance reporting of the prolonged jobless recovery, the
recession or depression (depends on who you are and where you live),
and the Eurozone issues, one of the more positive stories about the
global economy is the enormous economic growth in many emerging
markets (although it is beginning to slow in 2013). We have looked
at Brazil; now, let's take a quick look at China and India and the
opportunities that they represent.

According to a report by the BLS, in 2010, US GDP led the world at slightly more than $14 trillion. China occupied second place at around $10 trillion. Since 1990, China's share of global GDP has surged from 5% to 15% which has contributed to increased purchasing power for many of its households. Although not as large as China, India's GDP is also huge, and was ranked 4th in the world in 2010 at around $4 trillion[1].

If one starts with the broad assumption (which always has exceptions) that once households enjoy increased purchasing power, they will generally have similar demand and spending behavior (although not necessarily similar priorities) which generates increased consumer demand for a wide range of industries. Supplying this demand with relevant products or services is an opportunity for entrepreneurs and innovators, however, success is in the details: who, what, when, where, how. This applies to both foreign and local entrepreneurs. Foreign entrepreneurs and businesses can't simply tweak their brands—they have to make them relevant. Just ask all of the well-known global companies that have already stumbled or failed in their initial attempts to penetrate these markets (see Issue 21: Customer Relationships, and Issue 28: the Bottom of the Pyramid.)

For entrepreneurs and innovators, the next decade will be full of opportunities to provide products and services to the biggest new market in history. Consequently, the decade will also be very competitive, as all major and minor brands will be competing for market share. To be successful, think of ways to be hyper-relevant to consumers. Focus on providing smaller, cheaper, easier to use, more convenient, and higher-value products and services to a micro-market that you understand well.

## Example: Technology & Education

One key element that drives innovation and economic growth is a constant supply of well-educated science and engineering professionals. Part of the success of any rapidly developing economy, including China and India is the benefit received from a consistent pipeline of both locally and internationally educated science and technology graduates, especially those with advanced degrees.

Given that the US is a hub for advanced degrees earned by temporary visa holders, there is an ongoing debate in this country on how best to retain these foreign graduates to benefit from their education, skills, entrepreneurship and future innovation. In the global new normal, countries will become more competitive in trying to attract this valuable, well-educated talent pool. According to data from the National Science Foundation, in 2011, 36% of US science and engineering doctorates were earned by temporary visa holders. Graduates from China, India and South Korea represented about half of those US doctorates[2].

This scenario, however, does not have to be a zero-sum game in which the country that is selected by these valuable graduates wins and the other country loses. Some of these students may leave, but that doesn't mean they have to be forgotten. By establishing and maintaining a global network of friends, business & educational contacts, cultural understanding, multilingual capabilities, collaborations, and partnerships, multinational entrepreneurialism can flourish across multiple borders to create businesses and jobs worldwide.

## Entrepreneurs & Disruptors: "Chance Favors the Prepared Mind"—Louis Pasteur

One observation I hear from time to time is that despite the fact that India and China graduate several times more engineers than the US, these engineers don't receive the same quality of education as those educated in the US. As a result, many of these engineering graduates end up working in non-engineering jobs across several industries (not unlike recent US graduates who are unable to land jobs in their field).

From a disruptive innovation viewpoint, this scenario represents an incredibly fertile environment for startups. In a rapidly developing and dynamic economy, individuals with specific and unique training and perspectives randomly placed across a broad range of industries will have a valuable opportunity to identify and launch a myriad of innovative business models.

## Mix & Match:

Whether you are a foreign student educated in the US or in your home country, what are your areas of expertise, interests, or unique perspectives, and how can you apply them to address unmet consumer demand?

Mathematics

Entertainment

Computer sciences

Agriculture

Engineering

Retail

Physics

Finance

Design

Economics

Commodities

Others

# Your Ideas:

# Conclusion:

The 2012 presidential election is over and 2013 is well-underway. Now we wait and see whether we return to the pre-election status quo or move forward in a more collaborative, problem-solving, job-creating environment. The decision-making on the budget, and the effects of the "fiscal cliff" and the "sequester" will be good first indicators. However, we must also continue to focus on the challenges we face in this new normal of employment and job creation

The Great Recession in the US formally ended in June 2009, almost four years ago. Today, the US still has a formal unemployment rate of 7.6% and a startling alternative unemployment rate just under 14%. Many developed markets, especially in Europe, are struggling, and the explosive emerging market phenomenon is also beginning to slow—all of which can have a detrimental effect on employment.

Global economic, political, social and technological changes are accelerating, which require governments, institutions, companies, and individuals to constantly adapt to keep pace. This is especially important with respect to job creation. Unfortunately for many people, this adaptation process is not happening quickly enough. We can no longer continue to wait for or depend on others to replace all of those lost jobs and benefits packages. The hard truth is that some of the jobs lost will not be coming back, and some of the individuals who are the most directly affected and displaced must consider alternatives, such as retraining, switching industries, finding contract or part-time work, or, in some cases, becoming a full-time or part-time entrepreneur or innovator.

It is not important whether you consider the current environment to be a paradigm shift, the new normal, or just an uncomfortably long economic slowdown. What is important is that we recognize the challenges and opportunities and try to create for ourselves, our families and our communities some additional employment options. For many people, becoming an entrepreneur or innovator will not be easy, and there is certainly no guarantee of success. However, there is a growing infrastructure and network of individuals and resources available that can guide and support you throughout the entire process—you do not have to do it alone.

There is a world of opportunities out there for aspiring entrepreneurs—Take a look!

# Notes:

## Part One: Why: Structural Shifts & Employment in the "New Normal"

## Issue 1: US Employment: The New Normal

[1] The Federal Reserve of Dallas, Branding the Great Recession, by Thomas F. Siems, Financial Insights, Vol. 1, Issue, 1, May 31,2012, Web. April 3,2013 http://www.dallasfed.org/assets/documents/banking/firm/fi/fi1201.pdf

[2] The Federal Reserve of Minneapolis, The Recession and Recovery in Perspective, Chart: Change in Employment: Recoveries, http://www.minneapolisfed.org/publications_papers/studies/recession_perspective/ and Bureau of Labor Statistics, Labor Force Statistics from the Current Population Survey, http://data.bls.gov/pdq/SurveyOutputServlet

[3] Bureau of Labor Statistics, The Recession Of 2007–2009, BLS Spotlight On Statistics, Feb. 2012, Web, April 3, 2013, http://www.bls.gov/spotlight/2012/recession/pdf/recession_bls_spotlight.pdf

[4] Bureau of Labor Statistics. "Unemployed persons by age, sex, race, Hispanic or Latino ethnicity, marital status, and duration of unemployment." July 2012. Web. August 14, 2012. http://www.bls.gov/web/empsit/cpseea36.pdf, http://www.bls.gov/cps/duration.htm (based on the BLS raising its maximum duration of unemployment from two years to five years)

[5] Atkinson, R., Stewart, L., Andes, S., Ezell, S. "Worse Than the Great Depression: What Experts Are Missing About American Manufacturing Decline," The

Information Technology and Innovation Foundation, March 2012, p. 8
http://www2.itif.org/2012-american-manufacturing-decline.pdf

# Issue 2: The Real Unemployment Rate

[1] Bureau of Labor Statistics. "Labor Force Statistics from the Current Population Survey: Seasonal Unemployment Rate." January 2002–July 2012. Web. August 14, 2012. http://www.bls.gov/webapps/legacy/cpsatab1.htm

[2] Bureau of Labor Statistics. "Alternative measures of labor underutilization."
July 2011–July 2012. Web. August 14, 2012.
http://www.bls.gov/news.release/empsit.t15.htm.

[3] Bureau of Labor Statistics. "Unemployed persons by duration of unemployment."
July 2011–July 2012. Web. August 14, 2012.
http://www.bls.gov/news.release/empsit.t12.htm.

[4] Bureau of Labor Statistics. "Employed and unemployed persons by occupation, not seasonally adjusted." July 2011–July 2012. Web. August 14, 2012.
http://www.bls.gov/news.release/empsit.t13.htm.

[5] Bureau of Labor Statistics. "Employment status of the civilian population by race, sex, and age." July 2011–July 2012. Web. August 14, 2012. http://www.bls.gov/news.release/empsit.t02.htm.

[6] Bureau of Labor Statistics. "Employment status of the Hispanic or Latino population by sex and age." July 2011–July 2012. Web. August 14, 2012.
http://www.bls.gov/news.release/empsit.t03.htm.

[7] Bureau of Labor Statistics. "Regional and State Employment and Unemployment."
June 2012. Web. August 14, 2012.
http://www.bls.gov/news.release/pdf/laus.pdf.

# Issue 3: Manufacturing & Consumer Spending

[1] Atkinson, R., Stewart, L., Andes, S., Ezell, S. "Worse Than the Great Depression: What Experts Are Missing About American Manufacturing Decline," The Information Technology and Innovation Foundation, March 2012, p. 8 http://www2.itif.org/2012-american-manufacturing-decline.pdf

[2] Fleck, S., Glaser, J. and Sprague, S. "The compensation-productivity gap: a visual essay." *Bureau of Labor Statistics Monthly Labor Review.* January 2011. http://www. bls.gov/opub/mlr/2011/01/art3full.pdf and http://www.census.gov/prod/2012pubs/ p60-243.pdf,http://www.census.gov/hhes/www/income/data/historical/inequality/ IE-1.pdf http://www.census.gov/hhes/www/income/data/inequality/middleclass. html, and The Changing Shape of the Nation's Income Distribution 1947-1998, Web April, 9, 2013 http://www.census.gov/prod/2000pubs/p60-204.pdf, p60-204, June 2000

[3] The Federal Reserve Board, Household Debt Service and Financial Obligtions Ratios, Web. April 3, 2013, http://www.federalreserve.gov/releases/housedebt/ default.htm

# Issue 4: Automation & Outsourcing

[1] Wheelock, D.C. "Banking Industry Consolidation and Market Structure: Impact of the Financial Crisis and Recession." *Federal Reserve Bank of St. Louis Review.* November/December 2011, 93(6), pp. 419-38.Web April 11, 2013. http://research. stlouisfed.org/publications/review/11/11/419-438Wheelock.pdf

[2] Bolling, C. and Gehlhar, Mark. "Global Food Manufacturing Reorients To Meet New Demands." *New Directions in Global Food Markets.* USDA, 2005. pp. 69, Web April 3, 2013. http://www.ers.usda.gov/publications/aib794/aib794g.pdf

[3] Moncartz, R.J., Wolf, Michael G., Wright, Benjamin. "Service-providing occupations, offshoring, and the labor market." *Bureau of Labor Statistics Monthly Labor Review.* December 2008. Web. August 14, 2012. http://www.bls.gov/opub/ mlr/2008/12/art4full.pdf.

## Issue 5: Housing & Income Distribution

[1] Chakrabarti, R., Donghoon Lee, Wilbert van der Klaauw, and Basit Zafar. "Household Debt and Saving during the 2007 Recession." *Federal Reserve Bank of New York, Staff Reports.* No. 482, January 2011. Web. August 15, 2012. http://www. conference-board.org/retrievefile.cfm?filename=sr482.pdf&type=subsite.

[2] DeNavas-Walt, Carmen, Bernadette D. Proctor, and Jessica C. Smith. "Income, Poverty, and Health Insurance Coverage in the United States: 2010." US Census Bureau, Current Population Reports, p. 60–239. US Government Printing Office, Washington, DC, 2011. http://www.census.gov/prod/2011pubs/p60-239.pdf., http://www.census.gov/hhes/www/income/data/inequality/middleclass.html, Web, April 11, 2013 http://www.census.gov/prod/2012pubs/p60-243.pdf, p.8

[3] http://www.census.gov/hhes/www/income/data/inequality/middleclass.html, http://www.census.gov/prod/2012pubs/p60-243.pdf, Web April 9, 2013 http://www. census.gov/hhes/www/income/data/historical/inequality/IE-1.pdf., http://web. archive.org/web/20070626183417/http://www.census.gov/hhes/www/income/ histinc/p60no231_tablea3.pdf

## Part Two: How: Entrepreneurial "Engines of Growth"—Again

## Issue 6: The Age of the Individual

[1] Shane, Scott, "Failure Rates by Sector: The Real Numbers" September 24, 2012, http://smallbiztrends.com/2012/09/failure-rates-by-sector-the-real-numbers.html Census Bureau, *Business Dynamic Statistics. And* Census Bureau, *Business Dynamic Statistics*, Statistics of US Businesses Database, Web. April 3, 2013 http://www. census.gov/econ/susb/ and SBA FAQs, http://web.sba.gov/faqs/faqIndexAll. cfm?areaid=24 and US Small Business Administration, Advocacy Small Business Statistics and Research, FAQs, http://web.sba.gov/faqs/faqIndexAll.cfm?areaid=24

[2] Devries, Henry, Baru, Sundari, and Shapiro, Josh. "Hot Careers for College Grads and Returning Students 2012." UC San Diego, Extension. June 2011.

# Issue 7: The Entrepreneurial Revolution

[1] *Internet World Stats.* December 31, 2011. Web. August 16, 2012. http://www. internetworldstats.com/stats.htm.

[2] United States Census Bureau. "Number of Firms, Number of Establishments, Employment, and Annual Payroll by Enterprise Employment Size for the United States and States, Totals: 2009." 2009 County Business Patterns. Web. August 16, 2012. http://www2.census.gov/econ/susb/data/2009/us_state_totals_2009.xls.

[3] The US Small Business Administration, Advocacy Small Business Statistics and Research, FAQs, http://web.sba.gov/faqs/faqIndexAll.cfm?areaid=24.

# Issue 8: The Innovation/Usefulness Gap

# Issue 9: The 1% Innovation & Entrepreneur Fund

[1] Bureau of Labor Statistics. "Labor Force Statistics from the Current Population Survey: (Seas) Civilian Labor Force Level." Jan. 2002–July 2012. Web. December 10, 2012. http://www.bls.gov/webapps/legacy/cpsatab1.htm

[2] Bureau of Labor Statistics. "Alternative measures of labor underutilization." July 2011–July 2012. Web. December 10, 2012. http://www.bls.gov/news.release/empsit. t15.htm

[3] Federal Reserve statistical release, Flow of Funds Accounts of the US, p.70, March 7th, 2013, Web April3, 2013. http://www.federalreserve.gov/releases/z1/ Current/z1.pdf,

[4] Henry, James S, Tax Justice Network. "The Price of Offshore Revisited: Press Release." *Estimating the Price of Offshore.* July 19, 2012. Web. August 16, 2012. http://www.taxjustice.net/cms/upload/pdf/The_Price_of_Offshore_Revisited_ Presser_120722.pdf.

[5] Henry, James S., Tax Justice Network. "Revised Estimates of Private Banking Assets Under Management and Total Client Assets—Top 50 Global Private Banks,

2005–2010." *Estimating the Price of Offshore.* July 21, 2012. Web. August 16, 2012. http://www.taxjustice.net/cms/upload/pdf/Private%20Banking%202012.pdf.

[6] Fairly, Robert W. "Kauffman Index of Entrepreneurial Activity: 1996–2011." March, 2012. Web. August 16, 2012. http://www.kauffman.org/uploadedfiles/kiea_2012_report.pdf.

[7] Knopp, Linda. *2006 State of the Business Incubation Industry.* Athens, Ohio: NBIA Publications, 2007, via National Business Incubator Association. "Business Incubator FAQ." 2006. Web. August 16, 2012. http://www.nbia.org/resource_library/faq/#3.

# Part Three: What: US Issues & Trends for Entrepreneurs & Disruptors

# Issue 10: High School Graduation Rates

[1] Stillwell, R., and Sable, J. (2013). *Public School Graduates and Dropouts from the Common Core of Data: School Year 2009–10: First Look (Provisional Data)* (NCES 2013-309). U.S. Department of Education. Washington, DC: National Center for Education Statistics. http://nces.ed.gov/pubsearch.Web. April 4, 2013 http://nces.ed.gov/pubs2013/2013309.pdf

[2] Ibid.

[3] Bureau of Labor Statistics. "Employment status of the civilian population 25 years and over by educational attainment," July 2011–July 2012. Web. August 17, 2012. http://www.bls.gov/webapps/legacy/cpsatab4.htm.

[4] Bridgeland, John, M., John J. DiIulio, Jr., and Karen Burke Morison. "The Silent Epidemic: Perspectives of High School Dropouts." Civic Enterprises, Peter D. Hart Research Associates for the Bill & Melinda Gates Foundation, 2006. Web. August 17, 2012. http://www.gatesfoundation.org/united-states/Documents/TheSilentEpidemic3-06FINAL.pdf.

*Notes:*

[5] Alliance for Excellent Education. "High School Dropouts in America: Fact Sheet, 2010." Web. August 17, 2012. http://www.all4ed.org/files/GraduationRates_FactSheet.pdf.

[6] National Center for Education Statistics. "Number and percentage of public and private school teacher stayers, movers, and leavers: Various school years 1988–89 through 2008–09." Web. August 17, 2012. http://nces.ed.gov/programs/coe/tables/table-tat-1.asp.

[7] National Institutes of Nuerological Disorders and Stroke, ,DCDC2: Demystifying and Decoding Dyslexia, National Institutes of Health, February 28, 2006 http://www.ninds.nih.gov/news_and_events/news_articles/news_article_dyslexia_DCDC2.htm

[8] Sondik, Edward, J., Madans, Jennifer, H., Gentlemen, Jane, F. *Summary Health Statistics for US children: National Health Interview Survey, 2011.* National Center for Health Statistics. Vital Health Stat 10 (254). 2011. http://www.cdc.gov/nchs/fastats/adhd.htm

[9] OECD, *PISA 2009 Database.* 12 http://dx.doi.org/10.1787/888932343342, and Web, April 4, 2013 http://www.oecd.org/pisa/46643496.pdf, http://www.oecd.org/pisa/pisaproducts/

# Issue 11: The Baby Boomer Market

[1] United States Census Bureau. "2010 Census Shows Nation's Population Is Aging." May 26, 2011. Web. August 20, 2012. http://www.census.gov/newsroom/releases/archives/2010_census/cb11-cn147.html.

[2] Vincent, Grayson K. and Victoria A. Velkoff, 2010, *THE NEXT FOUR DECADES, The Older Population in the United States: 2010 to 2050*, Current Population Reports, P25-1138, U.S. Census Bureau, Washington, DC. Web, April 14, 2013 http://www.census.gov/prod/2010pubs/p25-1138.pdf

[3] Love, Jeffery, "Approaching 65: A Survey of Baby Boomers Turning 65 Years Old." *AARP*. December 2010. Web. August 20, 2012, http://assets.aarp.org/rgcenter/general/approaching-65.pdf.

## Issue 12: Extreme Weather

[1] NOAA National Climatic Data Center. "State of the Climate: National Overview for June 2012." July 2012. Web. August 20, 2012. http://www.ncdc.noaa.gov/sotc/national/2012/6.

[2] NOAA National Climatic Data Center. "NCDC 2010 Annual State of the Climate Report—Supplemental Figures and Information." January 12, 2011. Web. August 20, 2012. http://www.noaanews.noaa.gov/stories2011/20110112_globalstats_sup.html.

[3] Ericksen, P., Thornton, P., Notenbaert, A., Cramer, L., Jones, P. and Herrero, M. "Mapping hotspots of climate change and food insecurity in the global tropics." CCAFS Report 5. Copenhagen, Denmark: CCAFS, 2011.

## Issue 13: Habla Español?

[1] Ennis, Sharon R., Merarys Ríos-Vargas, and Nora G. Albert. "The Hispanic Population: 2010, 2010 Census Briefs." May 2011. Web. August 20, 2012. www.census.gov/prod/cen2010/briefs/c2010br-04.pdf.

[2] US Census Bureau, *U.S. Census Bureau Projections Show a Slower Growing, Older, More Diverse Nation a Half Century from Now*, Press Release, December 12, 2012, Web April 12, 2013, https://www.census.gov/newsroom/releases/archives/population/cb12-243.html

[3] Ennis, Sharon R., Merarys Ríos-Vargas, and Nora G. Albert. "The Hispanic Population: 2010, 2010 Census Briefs." May 2011. Web. August 20, 2012. www.census.gov/prod/cen2010/briefs/c2010br-04.pdf.

## Issue 14: Disruptive Innovation

[1] Christensen, Clayton M., *The Innovator's Dilemma: When New Technologies Cause Great Firms to Fail*. Boston: Harvard Business School Press, 1997.

*Notes:*

# Issue 15: Healthcare: New Ideas Needed—Stat

[1] Todd, Susan R. and Sommers, Benjamin D. Overview of the Uninsured in the United States: A Summary of the 2012 Current Population Survey Report, ASPE Issue Brief September 12, 2012, Web April 4, 2013, http://aspe.hhs.gov/health/reports/2012/uninsuredintheus/ib.shtml

[2] http://www.whitehouse.gov/blog/2012/06/28/ supreme-court-upholds-president-obamas-health-care-reform

[3] DeNavas-Walt, Carmen, Bernadette D. Proctor, and Jessica C. Smith. "Income, Poverty, and Health Insurance Coverage in the United States: 2010." US Census Bureau, Current Population Reports, p. 60–239. US Government Printing Office, Washington, DC, 2011. http://www.census.gov/prod/2011pubs/p60-239.pdf.

[4] OECD, *Health at a Glance 2011: OECD Indicators*, Web April 3, 2013 http://www.oecd.org/unitedstates/49084355.pdf

[5] Cohen, S. and Yu, W., *The Concentration and Persistence in the Level of Health Expenditures over Time: Estimates for the US Population, 2008–2009*, January 2012, Agency for Healthcare Research and Quality, Medical Expenditure Panel Survey, STATISTICAL BRIEF #354. http://meps.ahrq.gov/mepsweb/data_files/publications/st354/stat354.shtml, and Mark W. Stanton, M.A., *The High Concentration of US Health Care Expenditures*, Agency for Healthcare Research and Quality, US Dept. of Health & Human Services.http://www.ahrq.gov/research/ria19/expendria.htm

[6] NIHCM Foundation. "Understanding US Health Care Spending." NIHCM Foundation Data Brief. July, 2011. Web. August 20, 2012. http://nihcm.org/images/stories/NIHCM-CostBrief-Email.pdf.

# Issue 16: The Age of Thrift

[1] McCarthy, J. *Services Expenditures in This Business Cycle*, July 6, 2011, Federal Reserve Ban of New York, Web. April 4, 2013, http://libertystreeteconomics.newyorkfed.org/2011/07/discretionary-services-expenditures-in-this-business-cycle.html

[2] Agriculture and Agri-Food Canada. "Overview of the Retail Dollar Store Market in the United States—Opportunities for Canadian Agri-Food Exporters." May 2011. Web. August 20, 2012. http://www.ats.agr.gc.ca/amr/4356-eng.htm.

# Issue 17: Local Food

[1] Martinez, Steve, et al. "Local Food Systems: Concepts, Impacts, and Issues." ERR 97, US Department of Agriculture, Economic Research Service, May 2010. Web. August 20, 2012. http://www.ers.usda.gov/media/122868/err97_1_.pdf.

[2] United States Department of Agriculture. "US food import volume, by food group." 1999–2010. Web. August 20, 2012. http://www.ers.usda.gov/Data/foodimports/. and http://www.ers.usda.gov/datafiles/US_Food_Imports/Value_of_US_food_imports_by_food_group_/food2_1_.xls

[3] American Community Gardening Association. "Frequently Asked Questions." Web. August 20, 2012. http://www.communitygarden.org/learn/faq.php.

# Issue 18: Web & Mobile Business

[1] *Internet World Stats*. December 31, 2011. Web. August 16, 2012. http://www.internetworldstats.com/stats.htm.

[2] "Top Sites in United States." Alexa: The Web Information Company. Web. August 20, 2012. http://www.alexa.com/topsites/countries/US.

[3] National Economics Council, *Entrepreneurship and the Global Economy* "*Entrepreneurship and the Global Economy*" Remarks at the Presidential Summit on Entrepreneurship Lawrence H. Summers, April 27, 2010, Web April 4, 2013, http://www.whitehouse.gov/administration/eop/nec/speeches/entrepreneurship-global-economy

[4] "Top Sites. Global" Alexa: *The Web Information Company*. Web. August 20, 2012. http://www.alexa.com/topsites.

# Issue 19: Co-ops, Barter, P2P, & Crowd Sourcing

[1] "About Co-ops." National Cooperative Business Association. 2011. Web. August 20, 2012. http://www.ncba.coop/ncba/about-co-ops.

[2] *"Co-op Research/Economic Impact." National Cooperative Business Association. 2011. Web. August 20, 2012.* http://www.ncba.coop/ncba/about-co-ops/research-economic-impact.

[3] *International Year of Cooperatives 2012.* Web. August 20, 2012. http://social.un.org/coopsyear/.

[4] Mills, Cliff. and Davies, Will. and Planning Work Group of the International Co-operative Alliance, *Blueprint for a Co-operative Decade*, Centre for Mutual and Employee-owned Business, University of Oxford. January, 2013, Web April 4, 2013, http://ica.coop/sites/default/files/media_items/ICA%20Blueprint%20-%20Final%20version%20issued%207%20Feb%2013.pdf and *Gardner, Gary. "Emerging Co-operatives." Vital Signs*, World Watch Institute, February 22, 2012. Web. August 20, 2012. http://vitalsigns.worldwatch.org/vs-trend/emerging-co-operatives.

[5] http://www.govtrack.us/congress/bills/112/hr3606/text

[6] http://www.kickstarter.com/

# Issue 20: Cities & Towns—Reinvent Yourselves

[1] National Broadband Plan, Connecting America, Federal Communications Commission, Broadband.gov, Web. April 5, 2013 http://www.broadbandmap.gov/rank/all/state/percent-population/within-nation/speed-download-greater-than-3mbps-upload-greater-than-0.768mbps/ascending/

[2] "What Is Business Incubation?" National Business Incubation Association. Web. August 20, 2012. http://www.nbia.org/resource_library/what_is/index.php.

[3] Feld, Brad. *Startup Communities – Building an Entrepreneurial Ecosystem in Your City*. Hoboken: John Wiley & Sons, Inc., 2012

# Issue 21: Customer Relationships—The Core of Your Business?

# Issue 22: Big Challenges—Big Ideas—Big Opportunities

[1] American Society of Civil Engineers. "2013 Report Card for America's Infrastructure." 2013,. Web. April 6, 2013, http://www.infrastructurereportcard.org/ and http://www.infrastructurereportcard.org/grades/

[2] OECD, *PISA 2009 Database.* 12 http://dx.doi.org/10.1787/888932343342, and Web, April 4, 2013 http://www.oecd.org/pisa/46643496.pdf, http://www.oecd.org/ pisa/pisaproducts/

[3] K. Davis, C. Schoen, and K. Stremikis. "Mirror, Mirror on the Wall: How the Performance of the US Health Care System Compares Internationally, 2010 Update." The Commonwealth Fund. June 2010. Web. August 20, 2012. http://www. commonwealthfund.org/Publications/Fund-Reports/2010/Jun/Mirror-Mirror-Update.aspx?page=all#citation.

# Part Four: What: Global Issues & Trends for Entrepreneurs & Disruptors

# Issue 23: Global Unemployment

[1] Tasci, Murat and Mary Zenker. "Labor Market Rigidity, Unemployment, and the Great Recession." Federal Reserve Bank of Cleveland. June 29, 2011. Web. August 21, 2012. www.clevelandfed.org/research/commentary/2011/2011-11.cfm.

[2] International Labor Organization. "Global Employment Trends 2012: Preventing a deeper jobs crisis." International Labor Office. 2012. Web. August 21, 2012. http://

www.ilo.org/wcmsp5/groups/public/---dgreports/---dcomm/---publ/documents/
publication/wcms_171571.pdf.

[3] Congressional Budget Office (CBO). "The Budget and Economic Outlook: Fiscal Years 2012 to 2022." January 2012. Web. August 21, 2012. http://www.cbo.gov/ sites/default/files/cbofiles/attachments/01-31-2012_Outlook.pdf.

[4] International Labor Organization. "Global Employment Trends for Youth 2012." International Labor Office. 2012. Web. August 21, 2012. http://www.ilo. org/wcmsp5/groups/public/---dgreports/---dcomm/documents/publication/ wcms_180976.pdf.

[5] Bureau of Labor Statistics. "Employment status of the civilian non-institutional population by age, sex, and race." July 2012. Web. August 21, 2012. http://www.bls. gov/web/empsit/cpseea13.pdf.

# Issue 24: Top 10 Entrepreneurial Nations

[1] Acs, Zoltan J. and Szerb, Laszlo, "The 2012 Global Entrepreneurship and Development Index (GEDI): Perspectives from the Americas," GMU-CEPP GEDI 2012 Launch, 1/5/2012, The Heritage Foundation, http://eagle.gmu.edu/ newsroom/files/GEDI.pdf

# Issue 25: Water Management

[1] United Nations Environment Programme (UNEP), World Water Assessment Programme (WWAP), http://www.unwater.org/statistics_res.html

[2] Ibid.

[3] Ibid.

[4] WaterSense, Indoor Water Use in the US, US Environmental Protection Agency, http://www.epa.gov/WaterSense/pubs/indoor.html

[5] "Global WASH Facts." Centers for Disease Control. May 24, 2012. Web. August 21, 2012. http://www.cdc.gov/healthywater/global/wash_statistics.html

[6] Texas Water Development Board, FAQs, Web. April 6, 2013, http://www.twdb. texas.gov/innovativewater/desal/faq.asp#title-17 and http://www.twdb.texas.gov/ innovativewater/desal/faqseawater.asp

# Issue 26: Brazil—Emerging Middle Class & World-Class Events

[1] World Factbook, 2009. Washington D.C: China, India, Brazil, Russia., Population, Central Intelligence Agency, 2009, Web. August 21, 2012. https://www.cia.gov/ library/publications/the-world-factbook/index.html.

[2] Brazil's Middle Class in Numbers, Press Release, Brazil.,gov.br., Web April 7, 2013, http://www.brasil.gov.br/para/press/press-releases/august-1/ brazils-middle-class-in-numbers

[3] World Factbook, 2009. Washington D.C: Brazil, Major Cities Population, Central Intelligence Agency, 2009, Web. August 21, 2012. https://www.cia.gov/library/ publications/the-world-factbook/geos/br.html.

[4] Brazil's Middle Class in Numbers, Press Release, Brazil.,gov.br., Web April 7, 2013, http://www.brasil.gov.br/para/press/press-releases/august-1/ brazils-middle-class-in-numbers

[5] Torres, Helen Trouten. "Rio World Cup and Olympic Legacy: Economics." *The Rio Times.* September 13, 2011. Web. August 21, 2012. http://riotimesonline. com/brazil-news/rio-business/rio%E2%80%99s-world-cup-and-olympic- legacy-economics/#. And http://riotimesonline.com/brazil-news/front-page/ transport-funds-secured-for-rio-2016/

[6] World Factbook, 2009. Washington D.C: Brazil, Demographic Profile, Central Intelligence Agency, 2009, Web. August 21, 2012. https://www.cia.gov/library/ publications/the-world-factbook/geos/br.html.

[7] Ibid, Telephones: Mobile-Cellular

[8] US Energy Information Administration, Brazil, Analysis –Background, Web April 7, 2013, http://www.eia.gov/countries/cab.cfm?fips=BR

*Notes:*

# Issue 27: Global Competitiveness

[1] Schwab, Klaus, Xavier Sala-i-Martin, and Robert Greenhill. "The Global Competitiveness Report 2010–2011." World Economic Forum. 2010. Web. August 21, 2012. http://www3.weforum.org/docs/WEF_GlobalCompetitivenessReport_2010-11.pdf.

[2] National Science Board, *Research and Development: Essential Foundation for US Competitiveness in a Global Economy*. A Companion to Science and Engineering Indicators 2008 http://www.nsf.gov/statistics/nsb0803/start.htm

[3] "Doing Business 2011: Making a Difference for Entrepreneurs." The World Bank, the International Finance Corporation, 2010. Web. August 21, 2012. http://www.doingbusiness.org/~/media/FPDKM/Doing%20Business/Documents/Annual-Reports/English/DB11-FullReport.pdf. .

# Issue 28: Markets at the Bottom of the Pyramid

[1] World Resource Institute. "The Next 4 Billion: Market Size and Business Strategy at the Base of the Pyramid." International Finance Corporation. 2007. Web. August 21, 2012. http://pdf.wri.org/n4b_executive_summary_graphics.pdf.

[2] Prahalad, C.K. *The Fortune at the Bottom of the Pyramid—Eradicating Poverty Through Profits.* Upper Saddle River, NJ: Prentice Hall, 2005

# Issue 29: Social Entrepreneurs

[1] US AID, Millennium Development Goals, Results and Data, Web April 7, 2013, http://www.usaid.gov/mdg

[2] "Topics." The World Bank. Web. August 21, 2012., http://data.worldbank.org/topic.

# Issue 30: India & China: Emerging Giants

[1] Crofoot, Elizabeth, Kirchmer, Jacob et al., *Charting International Labor Comparisons*, U.S. Department of Labor • Bureau of Labor Statistics, September 2102. Web April 9, 2013 http://www.bls.gov/fls/chartbook/2012/chartbook2012.pdf

[2] National Science Foundation, National Center for Science and Engineering Statistics. 2012. *Doctorate Recipients from U.S. Universities*: 2011. Special Report NSF 13-301. Arlington, VA. Web April 9, 2013, Available http://www.nsf.gov/statistics/sed

Greg Smogard, PhD, is founder and CEO of 4catalysts consulting. He spent much of his career as an international business executive working with large, well-known, global brands in over 40 countries and in the US. He is also an advisor to a private equity firm, an investor, and an entrepreneur with experience managing his own start-ups. Mr. Smogard specializes in helping companies quickly improve their operations and increase their profits by enhancing relationships with existing customers, improving processes, launching new products and services, and identifying domestic and international business trends and opportunities.

He has lived and traveled extensively abroad. He speaks Spanish fluently, and he and his family currently split their time between the Dallas-Fort Worth area and Palos Verdes, California.

www.ingramcontent.com/pod-product-compliance
Lightning Source LLC
Chambersburg PA
CBHW070803280326
41934CB00012B/3040